MASTERING
AMAZON ASSOCIATES

Praise for *Mastering Amazon Associates*

"The true expert of the Amazon Associates program is Jesse Lakes! The tips, strategies, and pitfalls to avoid in this book are invaluable. I highly recommend any existing or potential Amazon Associate read this and follow its advice!"

-Spencer Haws
Founder, Niche Pursuits
Founder, LinkWhisper

"This is a great book! Quick read. Easy reference. Highly suggest you pick this up!"

-Jeven Dovey
Creator Film School
YouTuber

"I've known Jesse, and used Geniuslink, for years now and have always appreciated his ruthless curiosity and arcane knowledge around Amazon Associates. It's great seeing that come full circle now with all his expertise laid out in this book!"

-Lynda Mann
Former SVP of Commerce
Former Biz Dev at Wirecutter

"I've worked with the Amazon Associates program for years and this is the best book I've ever read on it. I've mostly been on the music and entertainment side of it, because that's the industry I've been in for more than a decade now. I've turned to this book dozens of times since reading it. Highly recommend this one if you're getting into it now. It's very relevant."

-Unknown Reader
Amazon.com Review

"5-stars! This book is a goldmine of info for any creator, especially writers. Understanding affiliate programs can be so confusing. This book breaks it all down into manageable chunks with specific instructions. I've already recommended it to all my writer friends. Don't miss this one."

-Rachel Thompson
Founder, Bad Redhead Media
Award-Winning Author

"It's well done and an exhaustive look at the Amazon affiliate program."

-Chris Guthrie
Founder, EasyAzon

Praise for *Mastering Amazon Associates*

"As a full-time creator, affiliate marketing is a critical revenue stream to my business. That said, I don't have time to stay on top of best-practices and compliance issues that could cripple my income. This book is a one-stop-shop that opened my eyes as to what I should (and shouldn't) be doing to maximize my revenue."

-Brandon Hassler
Founder, Tech Audit TV

"There is all sorts of info across the internet about Amazon Associates but this book is the bible!"

-John Brubaker
Speaker, Executive Coach,
Award-Winning Author

"Well done! The book reads fast and easily and it serves as a great intro to the program with lots of jumping off points."

- Doug Cunnington
Founder, Niche Site Project

"This book is like a playbook for beginners and experienced content publishers and influencers who monetize through Amazon Associates. This book will help prevent you from getting your account banned and give you the exact tactics to increase your affiliate earnings from your existing audience and traffic. After learning from Jesse, I realized I was leaving money on the table with my traffic. I implemented a few of the suggestions in this book and started making thousands more a month from my same traffic. Highly recommend it."

-Chris Yates
Founder, Rhodium Weekend
Owner, Centurica

This is simply the most incredible resource for anyone who works in Amazon Associates in any way. Jesse has done an incredible job of summarizing all of the tricks of the trade, policies, and other nuances of the Amazon associates ecosystem. The three things that stuck out to me the most from Jesse's book: First, he speaks in terms almost anyone can grasp, the sign of dominant knowledge. Second, he gets into the tactics that you need to know to win, and third, he does a great job of weaving in Amazon policies - which matter a lot.

-Ben Faw
Co-Founder/CEO, AdVon Commerce
Partner, Dynamism Capital
Co-Founder, BestReviews

MASTERING
AMAZON ASSOCIATES

A CREATOR'S GUIDE TO THE
AMAZON AFFILIATE PROGRAM

Jesse Lakes
& Team Geniuslink

Mastering Amazon Associates -
A Creator's Guide To The Amazon Affiliate Program

© Copyright 2023 GeoRiot Networks, Inc.

All rights reserved. No part of this book may be reproduced or transmitted in any form or by any means, electronic or mechanical, including photocopying, recording, or by any information storage and retrieval system without the prior written permission of the publisher, except for the inclusion of brief quotations in critical reviews and certain other noncommercial uses permitted by copyright law. For permission requests, contact the publisher.

Version 1.1 (June, 2022)
Version 1.2 (January, 2023)
Version 1.3 (June, 2023)

ISBN (paperback): 979-8986457208

Published by GeoRiot Networks, Inc. D/B/A Geniuslink
2320 S. Spokane St., Seattle, WA 98144
https://geniuslink.com
hi@geni.us

Written by Jesse Lakes
With special help from Team Geniuslink
Images by Matt Mustarde
Cover design by Matt Mustarde and Steven Sundheim
Supporting material from https://geniuslink.com/blog/
Printed by Amazon Printing On Demand / Kindle Direct Publishing

Amazon, Amazon Associates, and a variety of other Amazon related terms Copyright Amazon.com.

Thank you...

To all the authors, musicians, bloggers, YouTubers, entrepreneurs, influencers, and professional (affiliate) marketers who have helped our dream become a reality and continue to support us every day.

To the amazing team at Geniuslink who keep the bus moving forward day in, day out.

To my wonderful family who keep me healthy and sane.

A gift for you
Extended trial & credit for Geniuslink

NEW CLIENTS
2x Free Trial
Use Geniuslink for free (with unlimited clicks) for **30 days** for sending us an email help@geni.us.

NEW CLIENTS
4x Free Trial
Use Geniuslink for free (with unlimited clicks) for 60 days for sending us a pic of you with this book.

EXISTING CLIENTS
$15 Credit
Email us a copy of your receipt for this book and we'll credit the retail price of the book to your account.

EXISTING CLIENTS
$30 Credit Trial
Email us a photo of you with this book and we'll credit 2X the retail price of the book to your account.

Table of Contents

Introduction — xvii
My (Affiliate) Story — 1
What is the Amazon Affiliate Program? — 11
    What is affiliate marketing? — 13
    Introducing Amazon — 15
    Where does the Amazon affiliate program fit in? — 16
    What sets the Amazon affiliate program apart? — 19
    Related programs — 21
    Seller Networks — 27
    Amazon CPC — 29
How to Become an Amazon Affiliate — 33
    Which Amazon affiliate program should I sign up for first? — 36
    Signing up for the Amazon affiliate program — 39
    Next steps — 43
    An alternative way to get started — 45
    Affiliate links on YouTube — 47
How to Stay Compliant as an Affiliate — 51
    Cloaking links — 54
    Offline links — 59
    Mentioning prices (or availability) — 62
    Using star ratings and reviews — 63
    Asking for a click (or bookmark) on your affiliate link — 64
    Link to products or services — 65
    Not including an affiliate disclaimer — 66
    Additional concerns for social media — 69

Table of Contents

Gray areas in the Operating Agreement	70
How to Increase Your Commissions (aka Best Practices)	**73**
Search Engine Optimization	75
Multiple affiliate links	78
Comparisons	83
Building a community	85
International shoppers	88
Going Global With Your Affiliate Links	**91**
Is your audience international?	95
International Amazon affiliate programs	96
Where to start (and which programs to avoid)	97
Intelligent links: OneLink vs. Geniuslink	100
Next steps	108
Advanced Amazon Affiliate Tips	**109**
Broken Amazon affiliate links	111
Using multiple Amazon affiliate tracking IDs	114
Mobile Deep Links	116
A/B testing your affiliate links	119
Using multiple affiliate programs	121
Product curation via Kit	127
Are you under or overperforming?	130
Exit your Amazon affiliate business	133
Wrapping Up	**137**
Thank you!	139
Questions? Ping me…	139
What did we miss?	140

Table of Contents

Our gift to you	140
Best of luck!	140
Appendix A - Worldwide Storefronts and Affiliate Programs	**143**
Appendix B - Amazon.com Commission Rates	**147**
Acknowledgements	

Introduction

Introduction

Amazon's affiliate program, officially known as Amazon Associates, has been around for over 20 years. In that time, it's become the world's largest affiliate program and is still the program we recommend most often to new creators.

After nearly a decade supporting tens of thousands of authors, YouTubers, niche and authority bloggers, musicians, gamers, and social media influencers across our three platforms (Geniuslink, Booklinker, and Kit), my team and I have learned a lot that we are excited to share! This book is the result of years of internal notes, blog articles, and support documents the team has written.

Use this definitive guide as your roadmap in the world of Amazon Associates. Let me start you with best practices to accelerate growth while steering clear of simple mistakes that can get your account banned.

For those already going down the Amazon Associates rabbit hole, let us help you expand easily into international markets and leverage advanced techniques to gain even more traction.

Be warned! Before we dive in, it's important to note:

- This is not a "get rich quick" style book. Building a sustainable business around Amazon Associates takes time and effort (lots and lots of both from my experience).

Introduction

- No "Black Hat" techniques here. Everything we propose doing are things we've done ourselves or worked closely with clients to do.

- Things change. Amazon's ecosystem constantly evolves, as do their policies and approaches. What worked previously may not be a best practice in the future.

And a quick disclosure before we get too far in:

I am a little biased. I've tried a lot of services, and I've built a number of tools to be successful in the Amazon Associates program. In this book, the tools and services I recommend are the ones I've found the most success with and still use. Of course, the tools I've built are the ones I favor. Go figure, right?

I am the founder, dishwasher, head janitor, and ardent cheerleader for Geniuslink, Booklinker, and Kit. These are the main tools I work with, and the ones I will discuss in the most depth.

My (Affiliate) Story

* I don't actually look anything like our protagonist (his name is Geo)

My (Affiliate) Story

I'm a child of the 80s, which means I was graduating from high school and heading to college at the turn of the century; just as the dot com crash came barreling in and wrecked everything.

I have always been a bit of a nerd, and while computers were cool, it was really the internet that completely fascinated me. With my high school graduation money, I bought my first domain, and web hosting, which began my entrepreneurial adventure in the online space.

I started off by building websites for friends and family, but it was not until my junior year of college that I was introduced to affiliate marketing in earnest. Let me tell you, it wasn't an enjoyable experience.

During an entrepreneurship class in my Junior year, I presented a business plan for a website that I was already a year into building. I had forecasted millions in revenue in the coming years through leveraging banner ads that were paying out $60-$80 for every one thousand times they were seen (referred to as "CPM" - cost per mille).

Unfortunately, my financial projections were based on stale data and a couple of years late. The dot com crash had thoroughly crushed those sky high CPMs. This forced me to pivot toward using affiliate-based banner ads to monetize the site which paid out on sales rather than impressions. Hard as I tried though, the payouts from my efforts were nothing compared to the carefully built financial projection spreadsheets I'd done for the business plan.

Turns out I was not going to be an internet-based millionaire before graduating college (and I blamed it squarely on affiliate marketing).

A short time after my introduction to affiliate marketing I began my first deep dive into Amazon's affiliate program by monetizing links to Amazon products using Google's Adwords platform. By purchasing

My (Affiliate) Story

highly targeted keywords, and creating ads on Google Adwords, you could promote affiliate links to specific products, and as long as the commission paid was greater than the cost per click on Adwords, you came out on top.

I rarely came out on top, but it was a fascinating learning experience that helped remove my frustration with affiliate marketing and allowed me to better understand how valuable it could be when used correctly.

After finishing my undergrad, I made the move from one college town to another, to really take advantage of my five years of higher education. This meant working as a waiter, eventually a short stint as a sushi chef, and then five glorious years as a white water rafting guide. It was definitely a non-traditional post-graduation path but during my "off time," my passion for web-based ventures, leveraging affiliate marketing, continued in earnest.

After multiple failed web endeavors focused on restaurant reviews, real estate, and then travel; I finally landed on my first affiliate-based venture that actually worked—soundtrack websites focused on extreme sports films. I have always been passionate about extreme sports like skiing, snowboarding, and surfing, so the match was perfect.

I'd go to all of the film premieres, note down each of the songs in the soundtrack (thank you iPhone and Shazam!), then update my website to list out the soundtracks for each with affiliate links to iTunes and Amazon. It was the perfect combination of my passions and allowed me to make enough to pay for my season pass to the local ski area along with some new gear.

After working on these sites for a few years, I noticed a scary trend: my year-to-year traffic was starting to hockey stick and grow exponentially but my revenue was barely growing at all.

My (Affiliate) Story

My "Ah Ha!" moment came when I realized that skiing, snowboarding, surfing, and music were loved internationally and my websites were now getting visits from around the world, leading to the incredible growth of the sites.

My "Oh No!" moment came shortly after when I realized that my iTunes and Amazon affiliate links only worked for my US-based visitors.

A little digging showed that both iTunes and Amazon had country/region-specific storefronts that were designed to sell products in that specific country/region. Furthermore, each of these storefronts had its own, independent, affiliate program that only worked for that specific storefront.

This meant that a US-based link (which is what I had on my site) wouldn't work for someone in the UK. The UK-based person could only buy the digital song from the UK store (thanks Digital Rights Management!) and if I was going to get credit for that sale I needed to use a UK-specific affiliate program to send that UK shopper to the UK store.

Being confronted with this problem set me on my now decade-long course to build a "smart" link, that could automatically send people to a different destination based on their location (or device, language, date, etc.) in order to solve these issues.

Unfortunately, there wasn't much documentation about how the iTunes Affiliate Program actually worked. So, I did what any good nerd does, and dove deep into the rabbit hole to deconstruct it, emerging a couple of months later with a massive pile of notes.

With this new understanding, I went to my best friend and college roommate who had gotten a "real job" at Microsoft to write code after graduating college, to beg for his help in solving this problem.

My (Affiliate) Story

While he set to work on building out the first prototype of the "smart" links for my websites, I decided to take the advice of another long-time friend and began compiling my notes into what became a 160-page, professionally edited PDF walking through the ins and outs of the iTunes Affiliate Program.

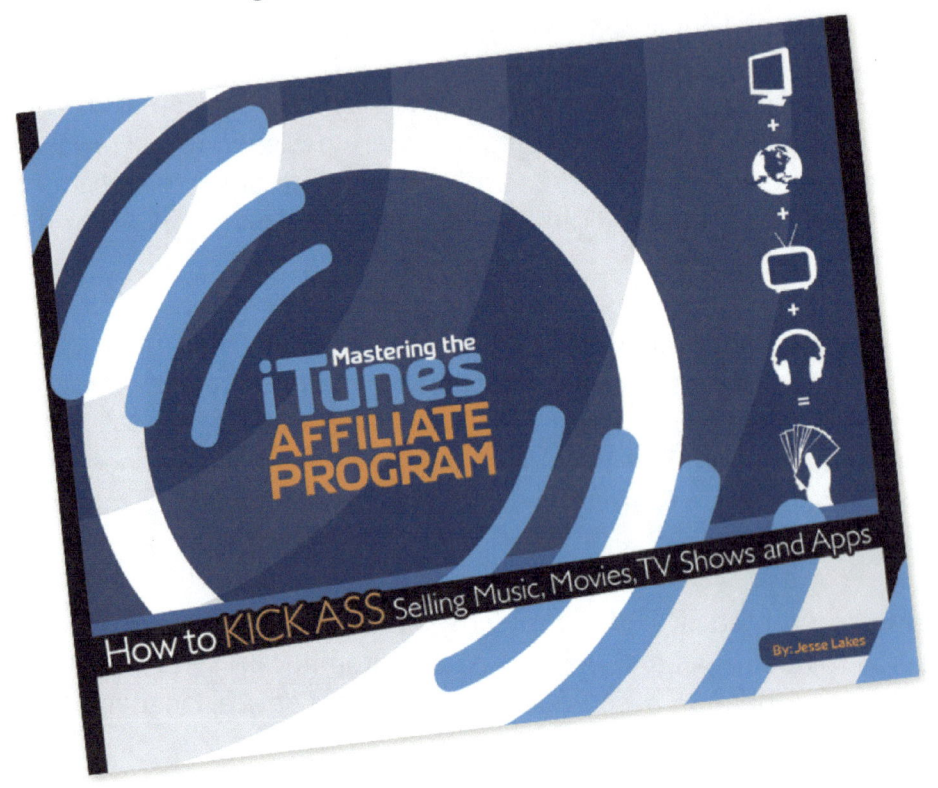

Before I officially "published" my ebook though, I sent a copy to a woman I'd found on LinkedIn who appeared to run the iTunes Affiliate Program at Apple. I thought she'd be excited about my hard work to create a comprehensive guide for her affiliate program.

Boy, was I wrong!

My (Affiliate) Story

Within a few hours of sending off the note, I was delivered what was essentially a "cease and desist" letter telling me not to publish the book, and letting me know the Apple legal team had been alerted. I was crapping my pants in fear.

Later that day, I found myself on a call with the head of the iTunes Affiliate Program. The call quickly turned from a nice civil conversation into a yelling match. She couldn't believe that someone, that they'd never heard of, could possibly know so much about their program. They were very concerned that publishing the book (full of lies they believed!) would ruin the program, etc.

Ultimately, we settled on letting her and her team take some time to review it and we'd talk again.

A couple of weeks later, I got a follow-up note and the tone had radically changed. While they had a few minor corrections, they were now curious if I'd consider working for them.

Hell yes!

It was a lifelong dream to work at Apple, so I quickly agreed to trade my flip-flops for a cubicle and a commute in Cupertino, California. (Jokes on them, I still wore flip flops daily for my first year of corporate life!)

Over the next couple years, my boss and I essentially made my book obsolete. One by one, we fixed the numerous problems I'd called out, published thorough documentation, and ultimately grew the affiliate program. After my tenure as the *Global Program Manager of the iTunes Affiliate Program*, we'd essentially tripled the footprint of the program from 17 individual affiliate programs to around 50 and nearly increased the amount of revenue coming through the affiliate program

My (Affiliate) Story

ten times. It was an amazing experience, and I learned a ton about how an international affiliate program is run.

However, as we continued to grow the affiliate program, it became clear we were making that same international buying and monetization challenge that had plagued my earlier sites worse. Like three times worse!

Similarly, Amazon was in the midst of global expansion as well and their affiliate program was "broken" with what we were now calling "geo-fragmentation."

In early 2012, after just over two years at Apple, I made the difficult decision to leave my day job and focus full-time on building out a better linking solution to solve geo-fragmentation across both the iTunes / Apple Services and Amazon ecosystems.

Drawing in my fiancée, who also previously worked at Apple, and that same best friend/college roommate who had helped me to solve the issue for my other sites; we built out a service called Geniuslink, formerly known as GeoRiot. For the past decade we have dedicated ourselves to solving the challenges creators and marketers face every day.

In that time, we've also been fortunate enough to acquire two similar platforms that are also focused around Amazon links: Booklinker.com and Kit.co.

The last ten years have been a total roller coaster. It has been incredible to see an idea, through countless hours of hard work, turn into a tool that makes a real difference in someone's life.

Today, I continue to lead the team at Geniuslink in our pursuit to help provide creators with the tools they need to monetize doing what they love most. Whether that's creating music, art, literature, films and videos, or even just sharing their thoughts on the best robotic vacuum, it is our mission to help them find success and navigate the tricky river of affiliate marketing.

- Jesse Lakes

What is the Amazon Affiliate Program?

Learn what affiliate marketing is and the basics of how it works.

Get a glimpse at the largest affiliate program in the world, Amazon's Associates program.

See the things that set Amazon's affiliate program apart from the rest.

→ *Even if you are familiar with affiliate marketing, or already signed up for the Amazon Associates Program, I would still encourage you to read through this chapter.*

What is affiliate marketing?

Before we dive into what the Amazon affiliate program is, we should probably start with the question "What is affiliate marketing?"

An **affiliate marketing program** is a way for a brand or retailer to extend the reach of their own marketing efforts by working with third parties to offer their products or services. In return, for their efforts, that third party would earn a commission or bounty on those sales.

Affiliate marketing is the term that covers all the processes involved with the tracking of referrals and sales, and then rewarding those who do so.

When I worked at Apple as the Global Program Manager of the iTunes Affiliate Program, I described our affiliate program to my office mates as an "infrastructure to facilitate partnerships," and I think that definition still holds true.

Affiliate marketing typically involves three major players:
- the brand or retailer (Amazon in this case),
- the person referring the shoppers (this is likely you, a creator),
- a platform that will track (often via a specialized tracking link), report, and enable payment for your efforts.

The way this works is that you, with a website, app, and/or social media channel, make a recommendation about a product or service while adding insights and value into the buying process for your community, and then follow that up with a specialized affiliate tracking link. Your

What is the Amazon Affiliate Program?

audience will then engage with your work and click on that link, be taken to the retailer, and, ideally, buy the product or service you recommended.

The retailer will see the sale was referred by you within a certain timeframe of the click and credit you for the sale at a predefined rate, often after the product has actually shipped to the customer. Finally, at some later point, all of those credits, minus any returns, will be paid to you.

With this success, you expand the recommendations and insights you provide to support a growing audience. Everyone wins--the shoppers get unique and additional insights about the products you use and discuss, you get rewarded for your time and effort, and the retailer is making additional sales it may not have made otherwise.

This simplification of the process ignores the sign-up, set-up, and payment aspects of the affiliate program. While those are important, they are administrative tasks that we will cover in the next chapter.

Beside the specific brand or retailer the affiliate program is built around, the next three biggest factors that differentiate an affiliate program are:
- the commission rates they pay out (often as a percentage of the sales price),
- how long the shopper has between clicking your link and making the purchase (often called the "cookie window"),
- how good is the store at getting you to spend money (this is often measured as the "conversion rate" but sometimes as "average order size").

Traditionally, these three values are rolled into the commissions earned and then normalized by the number of clicks it took to earn those commissions. This aggregates into what is the most important

KPI for an affiliate program: its **Earnings Per Click**, or **EPC** for short. EPC is a measure of how much money you earned per click through that affiliate link, or how effective each click you get on your affiliate link is.

EPC is calculated as your total earnings divided by your total clicks. Mostly! But there are two things to be cautious of:
- EPC was once calculated as earnings per 100 clicks. You don't regularly see this now, but be warned if something looks way off.
- Measuring clicks should be easy but you'll find that everyone does it slightly differently. If possible, when you are measuring EPC to compare affiliate programs, try to use a click count from an independent third party tool.

Introducing Amazon

Amazon was one of the early pioneers of affiliate marketing. The Amazon affiliate program launched in July 1996, making it over a quarter of a century old.

In that time, it's become the largest affiliate program in the world[1], with millions of affiliate publishers placing their specialized links across the internet to refer shoppers to Amazon's massive store.

Amazon's affiliate program was also an instrumental piece of its early growth. A Stanford report from 2008 claims 40% of sales for Amazon came from their Associates program[2]!

Over the last decade, we've seen Amazon's growth skyrocket and the share of traffic Associates contributes fall. Using SimilarWeb, one of

---

[1] https://geni.us/howbigisamazonaff
[2] https://geni.us/earlyamazon

the most popular web indexing tools, and looking specifically at Amazon.com and its referral traffic[3], the category where an affiliate would be classified, we see the following:
- 22% (Dec. 2017)
- 6.3% (Dec. 2019)
- 6.3% (Jun. 2022)
- 4.9% (Jan. 2023)

Where does the Amazon affiliate program fit in?

Amazon's affiliate program, officially known as **Amazon Associates**, is very similar to the tens of thousands of other affiliate programs out there and follows the model laid out above. In general, for sending qualified shoppers into an Amazon store via a specialized link, you will be rewarded with a commission on sales.

Amazon's affiliate program, called "Associates," is free to join.

While the process is generally the same, Amazon prefers to use its own terminology. What the industry calls "commissions," Amazon calls **Fees** and **Bounties**. They also call "affiliate publishers" **Associates**.

The big difference is that Amazon's affiliate program does not use an affiliate network, a third-party service that often provides tracking and reporting services to both the retailer/brand and the publisher. Amazon's affiliate program is managed "in-house." This is often the

---
[3] https://geni.us/referraltraffic

exception for how affiliate programs work as the majority of them use a third-party affiliate network.

Traditionally, the specialized affiliate tracking link for an affiliate program is long and ugly, as it includes multiple parameters and additional information necessary to make one or more redirects. However, since Amazon's affiliate program doesn't use an affiliate network, there is only a minor difference between a link you'd see in your browser while surfing around on the Amazon site and an affiliate link. That difference is the inclusion of the parameter "tag" followed by some characters that end with "-20" for Amazon.com. This additional info is often referred to as the "tracking ID" (but rarely the "store ID" when it's the default one for an account).

> Normal link:
> https://www.amazon.com/Martian-Andy-Weir/dp/0553418025/
>
> Affiliate link:
> https://www.amazon.com/Martian-Andy-Weir/dp/0553418025/?***tag=geniuslink-20***

The exception to this rule is when an Amazon affiliate link is shortened it can take the form of "https://amzn.to/..." where the ellipses is some random alphanumeric combination. The shortened "Amzn.to" link isn't necessarily an affiliate link but often is. The only way to know is to resolve (click on) the link and look for the "tag" and "-20" values in the URL.

Amazon's affiliate program, like the majority of today's affiliate programs, uses the **last-click attribution** model. This means the Associate who sends a shopper to Amazon is only rewarded if they are the last one to do so.

What is the Amazon Affiliate Program?

If, for example, you send a shopper to Amazon with one of your affiliate links, but before they buy, they go to another video and then click on the affiliate link in that description before actually buying, you lose out on the opportunity to earn a commission. While that other affiliate link, the last click before the purchase, will get credit for the sale.

Another way to lose out on commissions is for the "cookie window" to expire. The cookie window is the time Amazon allows for a sale to happen and still be credited to you. Amazon's affiliate program has a pretty tight window of 24 hours. So if someone clicked on your link, didn't click on any other affiliate links but waited 25 hours before they bought, you would miss out on the referral credit. Other programs can be much longer. Walmart, for example, offers 72 hours.

It's important to note that Amazon's cookie window isn't a measure of click-to-purchase but rather click-to-cart. As long as the product is moved to the cart within 24 hours, then purchased and shipped within 89 days, you'll earn that commission. This gives some extra flexibility but can also create some confusion in your earnings later down the road.

Finally, it's important to note that the **Amazon Associates program**, while often referred to as a single entity, is (as of May 2023) actually a collection of 20 public and two private independent and storefront-specific affiliate programs[4] (note that Amazon has been adding more and more storefronts and affiliate programs on a yearly basis and thus this number quickly changes). Just as Amazon has different storefronts for different parts of the world (e.g. Amazon.ca for Canada and Amazon.co.jp for Japan), each of these storefronts has its own affiliate program to support that specific store.

---

[4] See Appendix A for a breakdown of Amazon Storefronts and affiliate programs as of Jan. 2023.

In general, you can't earn commissions from the Canadian Amazon store using the Amazon.com affiliate program[5]. This is an important consideration when you have a global audience, and we'll dig into that more during the best practices section in the *Best Practices* chapter.

What sets the Amazon affiliate program apart?

There are three major benefits of using Amazon's affiliate program. While all three are related, the major benefits include: the program being easy to use, and high conversion rates.

The Amazon affiliate program is easy to use because it doesn't require the additional step of using an affiliate network, the dashboard is optimized, and there are minimal barriers to starting to use the program.

In fact, Amazon doesn't actually review your site until you've generated three sales. It is common for other affiliate programs to require you to verify your website or social media channel. One major network, AWIN, even requires you to pay a nominal fee before you can apply to any affiliate programs on their network.

amazonassociates

Thank you for applying!
You're now able to begin generating earnings with the Amazon.sg Associates programme. Once you **generate three qualified sales** within 180 days, our team will **review the website(s) or social account(s) associated with your application** to ensure that you are in compliance with the Amazon.sg Associate Programme Operating Agreement.

After signing up you have 180 days to make three sales before your account is reviewed.

---

[5] The recent addition of an "Earn Globally" initiative is starting to change this. More details in Chapter 2, "Signing up for the Amazon Affiliate Program."

What is the Amazon Affiliate Program?

The same factors that make the Amazon affiliate program easy to start also make it easy to use. Because of its huge size, there are numerous resources available including educational write ups, how-to guides, and easier access to experts (or at least those with experience who are happy to share). This also includes a sizable ecosystem of third-party tools and plugins that provide significant functionality "out of the box." This makes creating a relatively sophisticated setup fairly simple and well documented.

The Amazon affiliate program typically has a rather high conversion rate (see the *Advanced Amazon Affiliate Tips* chapter for more on this). Of course, this varies widely by your site or channel, the products you recommend, and your audience.

Amazon's affiliate program as a whole has three advantages compared to many other retailers that result in such a high conversion rate.

First, in the U.S., many people are comfortable shopping online with Amazon. EMarketer pegs its market share at over 40%[6], far ahead of many of its other e-commerce competitors (for example, Walmart is in the 4%-5% range). This familiarity with Amazon -- and even better, having an Amazon Prime membership (of which roughly 150 million Americans[7] are) -- means once you get a shopper into the Amazon store, your odds for a sale are high compared to sending a shopper to a store they've never used before.

Second, Amazon has a massive product catalog (roughly 350 million products across 25,000 sub-categories[8]). Amazon is the "everything store," and you can find almost anything for sale. This allows you to recommend particular products your niche would appreciate. Or,

---

[6] https://geni.us/emarketeramznmarket
[7] https://geni.us/primeusers
[8] https://geni.us/amazonstatistics and https://geni.us/amazoncategories

better yet, you can compare your preferred product to a few of the competing products to add even more value to the buying experience.

Third, in most cases, Amazon will pay you a commission for almost everything that is bought by the shopper you refer, even if it isn't the product that they clicked on in the first place. This can result in earned commissions from toilet paper and toasters, even if you sent them to Amazon for a specific TV or game. The earnings from the products sold that you didn't recommend are called **Halo commissions**, and Amazon tends to drive a higher volume of these types of purchases compared to other retailers because of their vast product catalog and people already being primed to shop there for everyday items.

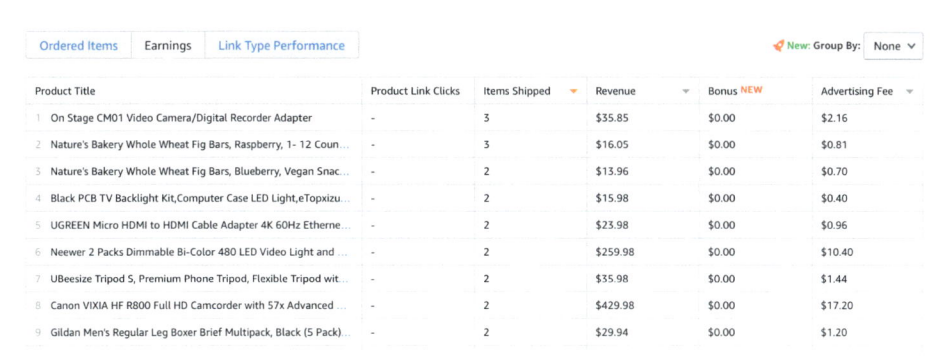

Lots of random stuff (like Fig Bars and boxer briefs?) being bought even though the focus is on photography.

Related programs

The Amazon Associates program is really a collection of three different programs:
- Offsite
- Onsite
- Influencer Program

What is the Amazon Affiliate Program?

The closely related **Amazon Attribution Program** is the foundation for **Seller Networks** which are essentially third party Amazon affiliate programs.

Finally, it's important to include the growing number of **Amazon CPC programs** that are an alternative way to monetize clicks to Amazon.

It's important to mention that these programs are not mutually exclusive, a publisher can technically be leveraging multiple.

The original Associates program, where creators share links to products from their various sites and channels, is now known as the **Offsite** version of the Associates program (as the affiliate links are being posted on other sites, thus "offsite" from Amazon's storefront). **The Offsite version of Associates will be the focus of this book.**

The **Onsite** version of Amazon's affiliate program, often referred to as "OSP" (On Site Program) ~~is~~ **was**[9] an invitation-only extension of the Associates program. The Onsite program is typically aimed at some of the largest publishers (think CNET, Digital Trends, and Wirecutter type sites) to take some of the product review-related content they've already written and allow for Amazon to post it within their site in exchange for still earning commissions from product reviews, though at a reduced rate in comparison to the Offsite program.[10]

---

[9] As of April, 2023 Modern Retail claims that OSP has been shut down. https://geni.us/ospdead
[10] https://geni.us/amazononsite

What is the Amazon Affiliate Program?

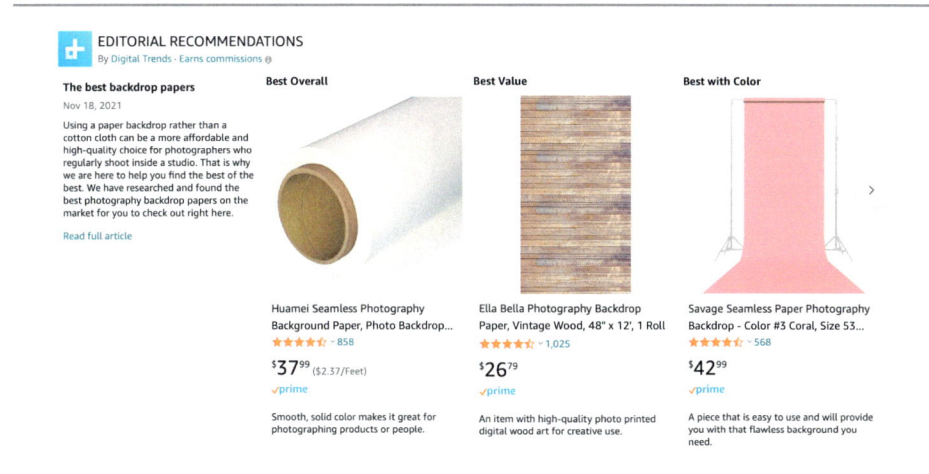

Deep in the search results on Amazon you might find a listing of products with endorsements from a publication outside of Amazon.

The **Amazon Influencer Program** is another extension of Amazon's Associates program that was launched in 2017. Targeted toward digital influencers and invitation-only, the setup is quite a bit different. Instead of picking and choosing the products you want to recommend from within Amazon's catalog and then sharing those individual product links across your site or channel, the Influencer Program gives you a space on the Amazon site to build your curation of products.

Influencers then share just a single Amazon link with their audience to drive them to their Amazon "storefront" (the landing page inside Amazon showcasing their curations of products), where subsequent sales result in commissions for the Influencer.

The content from an Amazon Influencer account can also, at Amazon's discretion, be used "Onsite" and intermixed with the product details page and search results pages.

What is the Amazon Affiliate Program?

Acceptance into the Influencer Program is based on a combination of your engagement metrics as well as followers on your YouTube, Instagram, or Facebook account and is storefront specific.

For those that are primarily posting their affiliate links on social media, the Amazon Influencer Program is a viable alternative to Amazon Associates, and some may find it easier to navigate.

However, there are some major pitfalls with the Influencers program. A few challenges include:

- The program is exclusive so continued participation is at Amazon's whim and at the expectation you keep your engagement metrics over a certain, unpublished, level.

- It's a newer program so we've heard that things change (and break) more often than with the Offsite program that is over 20 years old and much more mature.

- The Influencers Program's curated products lists has so far been storefront specific which leads to the same "geo-fragmentation" challenge mentioned in the *Going Global* chapter. By using Influencers with a global audience base you are alienating a subset of your audience and missing out on possible revenue with lost commissions.

What is the Amazon Affiliate Program?

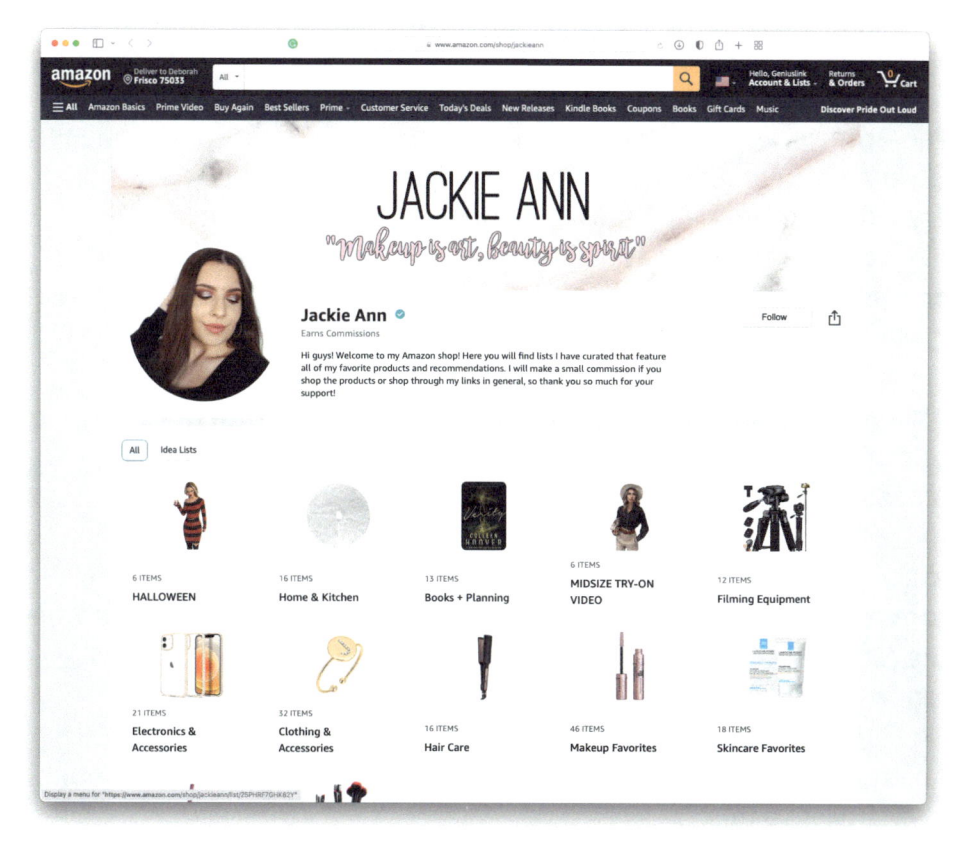

The Jackie Ann Amazon Influencer storefront includes collections of products that reward the influencer with commissions from sales.

The non-Amazon-specific tool that is also popular among influencers for sharing products is Kit.co. Discussed further in *How to Become an Amazon Affiliate* chapter, and again in *Advanced Amazon Affiliate Tips* chapter, Kit allows creators to curate "kits" of products around specific use cases to share with their audience, just like Amazon Influencers. However, Kit isn't Amazon-specific so creators can recommend products across various retailers and monetize their recommendations from multiple affiliate programs. Kit is also designed to support a global audience.

What is the Amazon Affiliate Program?

Full disclosure that we (Geniuslink) bought Kit in 2019[11] and have continued to integrate the two services ever since.

The **Amazon Attribution** program is managed by the Advertising team (a very different group than the Retail team who oversee the Associates programs) but the two programs are very similar. The biggest difference is that the Attribution program is targeted toward brands and sellers who sell products on Amazon's marketplace and are looking for insights about how well their marketing campaigns are doing with "external traffic" (e.g. driving clicks from outside to their products on Amazon). The Amazon Attribution program doesn't offer commissions for sales, but the links are formatted similar to an Amazon Associate link.

In short, the Associates program does a great job with paying out commissions but the reporting you can get from it is very limited while the Attribution program pays nothing but offers incredibly useful reporting.

An Amazon Attribution link often includes six parameters and would look similar to this:

```
https://www.amazon.com/dp/B08NXXXV4C?maas=maas_adg_api_590191837506986823_static_9_129&ref_=aa_maas&aa_campaignid=lv_yfeicZoDm4Cs3Yvhzl&aa_adgroupid=lv_PFUXi8qkMDf8qyZ2fs&aa_creativeid=lv_zjLM21xdgbFRTolEqI&m=AJ1I36VD0MUWL
```

---

[11] https://geni.us/geniuslinkkit

What is the Amazon Affiliate Program?

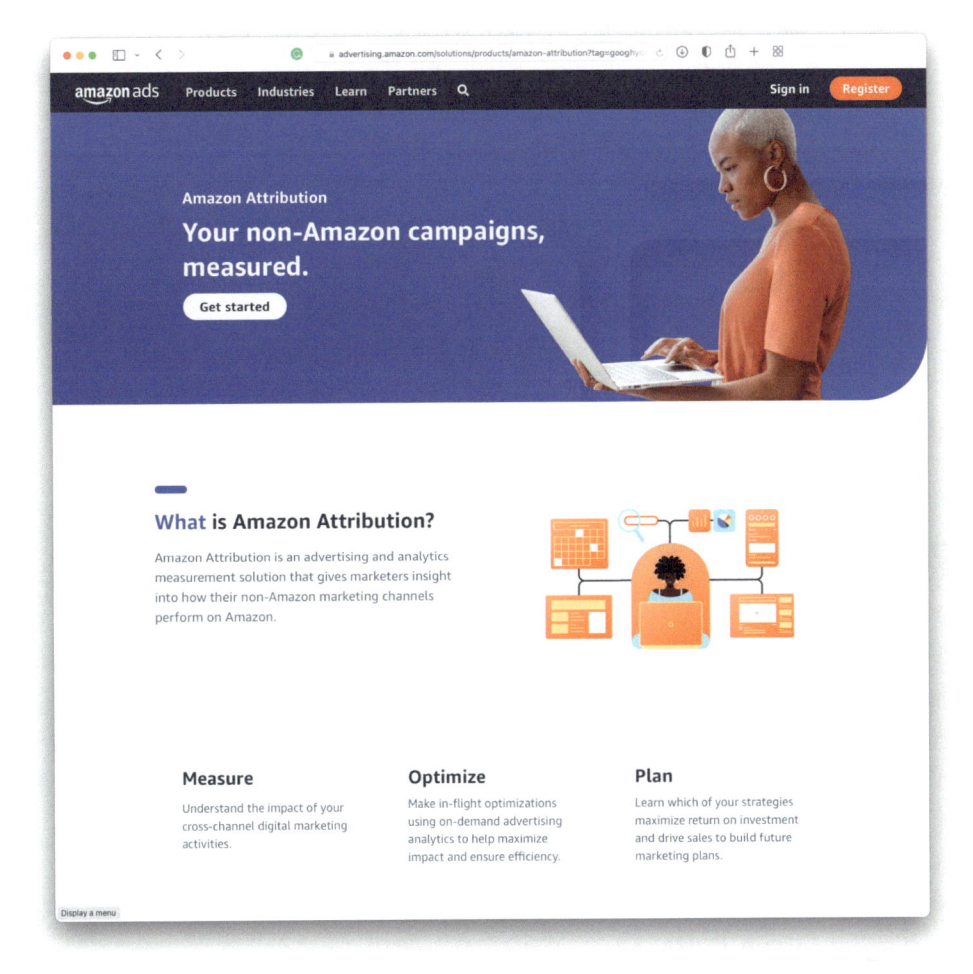

The Amazon Attribution program offers a lot of the same functionality as the (offsite) Associates Program but geared toward different marketers.

Seller Networks

The Attribution program recently came out of "beta" and in mid 2022 there was a significant wave of attention brought to the program, primarily due to an affiliate network by the name of **Refersion**, launching a "secondary" affiliate program for Amazon[12].

While not a new idea (**Publisher Expansion** and **DealMojo** offer a similar model and the now defunct RppleAnalytics was pushing this idea a handful of years ago), it's a very interesting one and something creators using the Associates program should be aware of, at least peripherally.

Amazon's Attribution program becomes the "tracking" layer to confirm which clicks result in sales, but then it's on the brands selling the products on Amazon to use some of their internal marketing budget to pay out the "commission" to the creator. This creates an interesting dynamic where brands have more control to offer competitive incentives that may be more attractive than what Affiliates will find in the Associates program.

Refersion, Publisher Expansion, and DealMojo each provide a platform to automate tracking sales, facilitating payments, as well as recruiting brands that commit to paying commission, and for creators to promote those specific products.

To date the biggest challenge is the limited number of brands and retailers opting into this type of arrangement.

In our estimates the total number of ASINS (the unique identifier that Amazon uses per product) supported by one of these networks is barely in the hundreds of thousands. Compare this to the hundreds of millions of total products that can be bought on Amazon, and monetized with Amazon Associates, and you'll see how the regular creator might not see much benefit from this set up (yet).

---

[12] https://geni.us/refersion

What is the Amazon Affiliate Program?

However, this space is getting lots of attention and expanding quickly. Our bet is on a new player by the name of **Levanta**[13], due to their deep experience in the industry around recruiting. However, **AdVon** is another player in the space, led by industry veterans of the Onsite Program, and is also looking really interesting. Full disclosure, Geniuslink recently invested in Levanta.

Besides the limited product catalog and multiple untested players in the space, the third major pitfall of using these **Seller Networks** is halo commissions are now limited to only other products sold by that specific seller on Amazon (which means those convenient sales of toilet paper won't count here).

The good news is our limited testing indicates one could build a link that leverages both the Amazon Associates program and includes the necessary Amazon Attribution parameters. So, technically, you can take advantage of both the commissions and halo commissions that can be earned from Amazon Associates as well as whatever commissions the brand or seller network offers.

It's early days here but it will be exciting to see how this evolves!

Amazon CPC

Another alternative to Amazon Associates is to use one of the growing number of monetization platforms that supports paying out on your clicks into Amazon. However, it's important to note that from our experience the pay out is often significantly less than what one might earn from (Offsite) Associates.

CPC (Cost Per Click), is typically associated with search engines not affiliate marketing. Instead of paying out on the action (as in CPA - Cost

---

[13] https://geni.us/levanta

What is the Amazon Affiliate Program?

Per Action), a CPC arrangement pays out per click. Note that you should ignore the "cost" part in both these acronyms as that is referring to the advertiser, not you the creator or publisher.

The CPC model is gaining attention due to the challenges with Last Click Attribution, the default model of CPA, benefiting publishers that are lower in the purchasing funnel (e.g. coupon and discount sites, buy now pay later service, etc.). CPC seems to better benefit the top of funnel types of publishers and creators who are focused on creating content and building awareness around a product.

The model also seems to be growing in popularity as the marketing teams at major retailers who were focused on advertising on search engines seem to be finding that the costs there have risen significantly and that they can find more return on the money they spend dedicating their budgets elsewhere.

Connexity (who were acquired by Taboola in 2021 but before that acquired Skimlinks in 2020) was my first introduction to a CPC payout for Amazon clicks. In 2018 it wasn't very interesting as the payouts were quite small, limited to only a subset of the Amazon product catalog, and the budgets were fixed. For us at the time this meant that of the very limited products that were supported at any given time, the earnings would fluctuate based on the season and payouts could be cut off abruptly if a campaigns budget was hit. It wasn't a very attractive model.

Five years later, new providers and a growing demand for CPC-based programs have led to us finding some reasonable solutions in the space. We haven't checked in on Connexity in a while but are enjoying what we see working with **Shopnomix** and **Kelkoo**. Additionally we've heard good things about **Noctemque**.

What is the Amazon Affiliate Program?

As it's a fairly new space for me please don't hesitate to reach out with other recommended providers or feedback. Thanks!

How to Become an Amazon Affiliate

Clear direction on how to get started with Amazon's affiliate program.

The details on getting signed up for your first Amazon affiliate program.

Best practices for signing up for international Amazon affiliate programs.

How Do I Become an Amazon Affiliate?

Initially getting set up with the Amazon affiliate program is fairly easy and shouldn't take more than half an hour. If you already have a site or community, then I encourage you to dive right into the next section and ignore the following few paragraphs.

However, if you are just starting out and don't yet have a website, channel, or an audience, then hear me out for a moment.

There are two schools of thought here. One is to build a community first, THEN start to monetize it via the Amazon affiliate program. The second is to sign up for the Amazon affiliate program very early in the process to ensure no penny is lost.

If you are brand new to all of this, then I would encourage you to take the first path and start working on building your site and community first before worrying about monetizing your efforts. I say this for a few reasons:

- While seeing the financial upside of your project can be incredibly rewarding, it can also be very distracting and disheartening early on if you are not seeing any commissions or clicks coming through. I would recommend you focus first on your craft and spend some time building whatever it is you plan on building. Once you've started to put out some content, are enjoying yourself, and are getting some engagement, then it's time to start monetizing -- not before.

- Amazon doesn't review your account until you've generated three sales, and you have 180 days to do so. If you fail to do this within that time frame, you risk having your account closed, which renders your previous affiliate links worthless and creates added work once you get a new account set up.

- Amazon recently changed how you can access their Product Advertising API, the tool that is essential for some of the more interesting Wordpress plugins and related tools (but not Geniuslink). Before this change, it was beneficial to get signed up with the program as soon as possible to get access to the Product Advertising API, but with this change, there is no added benefit to signing up early.

Which Amazon affiliate program should I sign up for first?

Now that you are ready to dive in and get signed up for the Amazon affiliate program, you need to decide which program to start with -- remember there are now 20 public Amazon affiliate programs[14]!

Start by going to the analytics of your channel/digital property and see where the majority of your audience is coming from. If most of your visitors are coming from the United States, then you want to start off with the Amazon.com affiliate program. However, if the bulk of your audience is coming from India, then Amazon.in's affiliate program makes more sense.

Ultimately, you'll want to sign up for all of the Amazon affiliate programs that match the countries where you see at least 10% of your site's, or channel's, traffic. We'll cover this further in the best practices section later in the *Best Practices* chapter.

It's important to note that initially you are not necessarily signing up for the Amazon affiliate program that matches the Amazon store you use or for the country you live in. Rather, you are signing up for the program that matches the store and country where the bulk of your traffic is from. It's a nuanced distinction but vitally important in

---
[14] See appendix 1

ensuring your initial efforts are as fruitful as possible. Regardless of where you live, you can sign up for most all of the Amazon affiliate programs.

The Associates programs for Brazil, Mexico, India, Egypt, and Turkey are a bit more challenging as some require a local address for signup while others aren't able to pay out commissions internationally. If you live in one of these countries I'd absolutely encourage you to leverage your local Associates program. However, if you don't live in one of these countries then you might want to wait.

More details about each of Amazon's Associates programs can be found in Appendix A.

You can easily get paid from most of the Amazon affiliate programs from almost anywhere in the world. Over the last few years, Amazon has made it very easy to receive direct bank transfers to over 50 different countries.

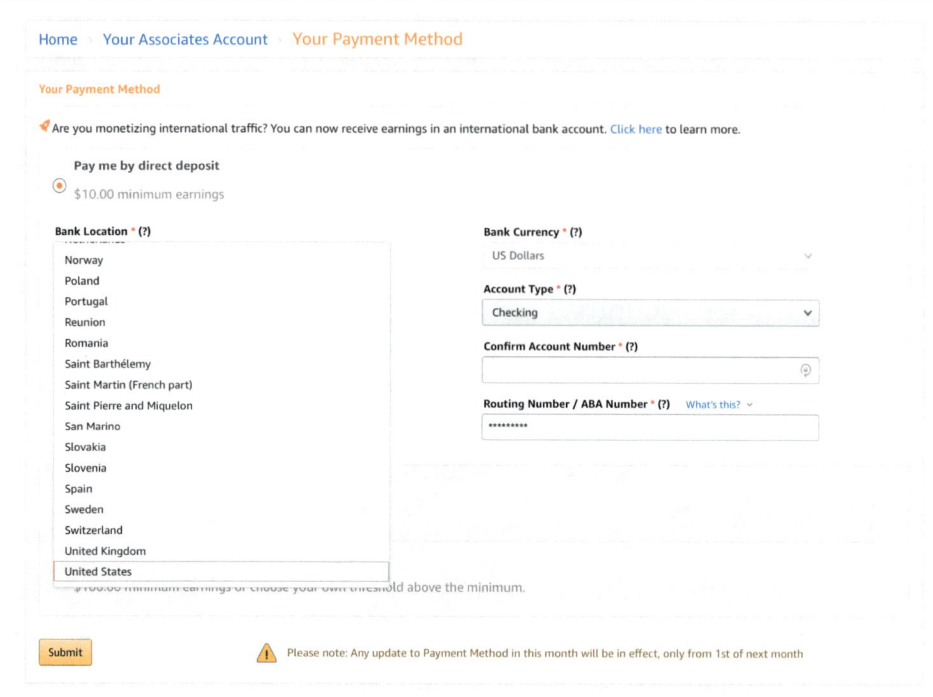

Inside the Associates Central dashboard, you can set up your payment method and choose direct deposit to be paid directly in approximately 50 countries.

If you are currently living in, or have a bank account based in, a country not currently supported by direct payments from Amazon you still have options:
1. Get sent a paper check, which will likely be in a foreign currency, and your bank might not want to deposit it (not recommended)
2. Set up a service like Payoneer, which offers international deposit accounts. You can learn more about how to leverage Payoneer to avoid the drudgery of getting foreign currency paper checks in our blog "The Amazon Associates Guide to Collecting International Commissions."[15]

---

[15] https://geni.us/intlcommissions

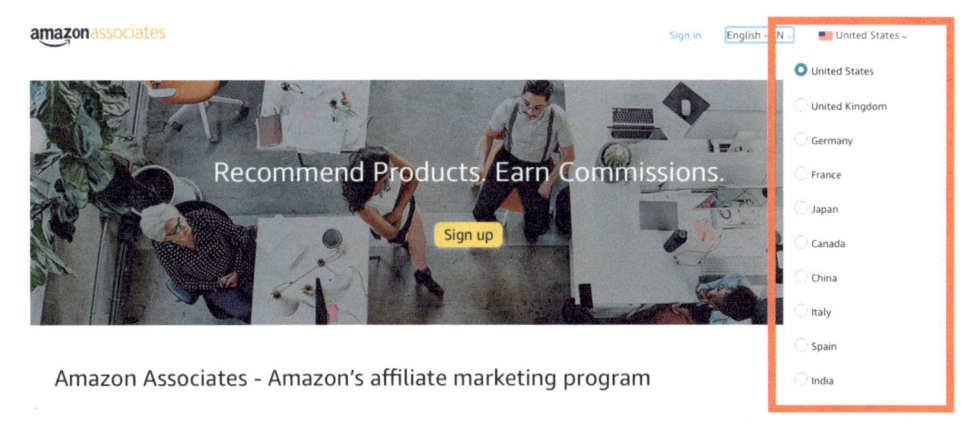

A quick note that you can easily jump between the public, region-specific Amazon affiliate programs via the drop-down in the upper right of any Amazon Associates Central dashboard.

Signing up for the Amazon affiliate program

Once you've narrowed down which Amazon affiliate program(s) you want to start with, it's time to dig in. For a video walk-through, please check out our recorded webinar on YouTube[16]. We also have a step-by-step guide[17] in the Geniuslink Knowledge Base to help you out.

Here are a few things to consider as you are signing up for the program:

Amazon.com's new Earn Globally program

In the spring of 2022 Amazon made a significant push forward in cleaning up some of the headaches associated with their affiliate program. In short, Amazon's new "Earn Globally" initiative allows you to earn commissions across additional storefront-specific Amazon affiliate programs through a single Amazon.com Associates account.

---

[16] https://geni.us/signupguideyt
[17] https://geni.us/signupguidekb

These six additional programs include the Canadian, United Kingdom, French, German, Italian, and Spanish Associate programs.

In late April of 2023, three more programs were added. These include Poland, Sweden and the Netherlands.

Now, with just a few clicks inside Associates Central, anyone with an Amazon.com Associates account can avoid the repetitive signup process for the nine other countries and easily save at least 20 minutes of their day.

Chrome vs. Foreign Languages

If you are applying for an Amazon affiliate program that is in a foreign language, then using the Chrome browser with built-in translation can be really helpful.

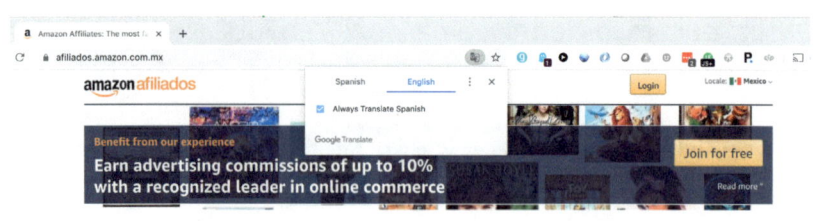

Chrome's built-in translation tools are a huge help in navigating an Amazon Associates Central and affiliate program sign-up process when it's in a foreign language.

UK + Four More

Somewhat similar to the Earn Global initiative discussed above, if you are signing up for the UK program, then at the end you'll be asked if you want to use the same information to automatically apply for four of the other programs in Europe. I encourage you to do this and save yourself some time (and fumbling around with foreign languages).

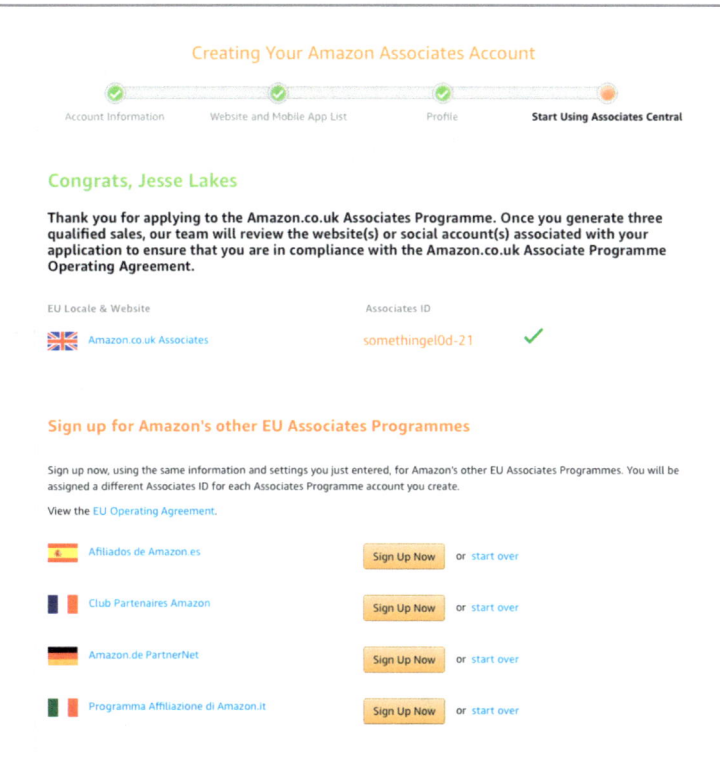

Viola! Five Associates accounts for the effort of signing up for one, thanks Amazon Associates UK for streamlining things.

Now vs. Later

Remember that any information you add now can be updated later. This means you can speed through fairly quickly, but on the flip side, it's important to keep your information up to date as your strategies develop and your portfolio and online presence expand. Forgetting to update the list of sites where you use your affiliate links can ultimately lead to getting your account closed!

How to Become an Amazon Affiliate

'Amazon Associates' via
ACTION REQUIRED – Your Amazon Associates Account –
To:
Reply-To: Amazon Associates

Hello

Your Associates account is at risk of closure.

Why?
We reviewed your account as part of our ongoing monitoring of the Amazon Associates Program. During our review, we determined that you are not in compliance with the Operating Agreement, found here: https://affiliate-program.amazon.com/help/operating/agreement.

- While reviewing your account we noticed that the information on your account, such as the identification of your site, is not current. Please ensure that the information associated with your account, including your email address, other contact information and identification of your site, is at all times complete, accurate, and up-to-date.

What Next?
Within five business days please correct the violations and notify us when you are in compliance through our customer service contact page: https://affiliate-program.amazon.com/home/contact. Please choose the subject 'Warning/Information Request Response' from the dropdown menu, and be sure to reference Issue Code in the comments field.

If you do not respond within five business days, we may close your Associates account and withhold commissions.

More information.
For more information about what we're looking for in your response, see our Warning help content, found here: https://affiliate-program.amazon.com/help/node/topic/GPPXH5WSX22AUNKR.

We look forward to hearing from you soon.

Amazon.com

Not keeping your list of websites updated or other pertinent info related to your Amazon Associates account can be grounds for getting it shut down!

While you don't have to fill out your tax and payment information when you are signing up, we encourage you to do so as soon as possible. While you won't be paid for approximately 60 to 90 days after you start earning commissions, it's always a bummer to delay a monthly payment cycle for forgetting to do something as simple as this.

Social Media Requires Full URLs

When filling out your website list during signup it's important to know if you are using affiliate links on social media, that you include the full channel or social handle when you list out your websites. For example, just listing "youtube.com" isn't enough -- they want to know the full URL to your channel. Not including this information can create a lot more hassle for you later.

Next steps

Once you've gotten signed up with your first Amazon affiliate program, it's time to build your first affiliate links so you can get them in front of your audience and generate those three sales so you can get your account approved!

There are lots of different ways to build an Amazon affiliate link. We'll quickly run through a few options for the three most common.

In Browser

The simplest way to build an Amazon affiliate link to share with your audience is to use Amazon's included "SiteStripe" tool that shows up at the top of your browser while you are on the Amazon.com site.

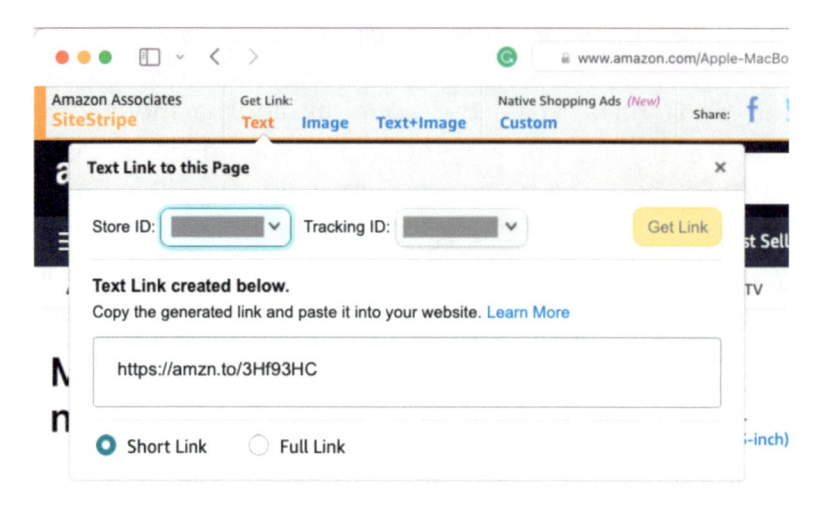

The Amazon Associates SiteStrip tool is handy but not very powerful.

There are multiple other browser-based plugins and extensions that can help you quickly and easily build an Amazon affiliate link. Our favorite of course is Geniuslink.

Your Website:

While a link generated from the SiteStripe or browser extension can be placed on your website, for WordPress-based websites, there are a number of plugins that can be really helpful to quickly build lots of Amazon affiliate links.

The two most common, and the ones I'm most knowledgeable about, include AAWP[18] and AmaLinks Pro[19] but searching for "Amazon Affiliate" on the WordPress plugin directory includes over 120 results[20].

Geniuslink also offers a WordPress plugin called the Amazon Link

---

[18] https://geni.us/aawpreview
[19] https://geni.us/amalinksproreview
[20] https://geni.us/wordpressplugins

Engine[21], which converts your regular Amazon links into globally aware Amazon affiliate links, so you can fully monetize your international audience and take advantage of multiple Amazon affiliate programs with a single link.

Link Management Tools

There are also a growing number of web-based link management tools that can help you create and manage Amazon affiliate links. This includes Geniuslink, along with many industry and genre specific tools.

A few worth mentioning include:
- **Pretty Links** with its focus around WordPress.
- **Books2Read**, **ReaderLinks**, and **Booklinker** (one of our properties) for authors and publishers.
- **Linkfire**, **SmartURL** and **Found.ee** for musicians and bands.

An alternative way to get started

An alternative approach to getting your first affiliate commissions is to leverage a tool like Kit.co or the Amazon Influencer Program. **Kit is designed for creators to share the products they love with their audience.**

---

[21] https://geni.us/amazonlinkengine

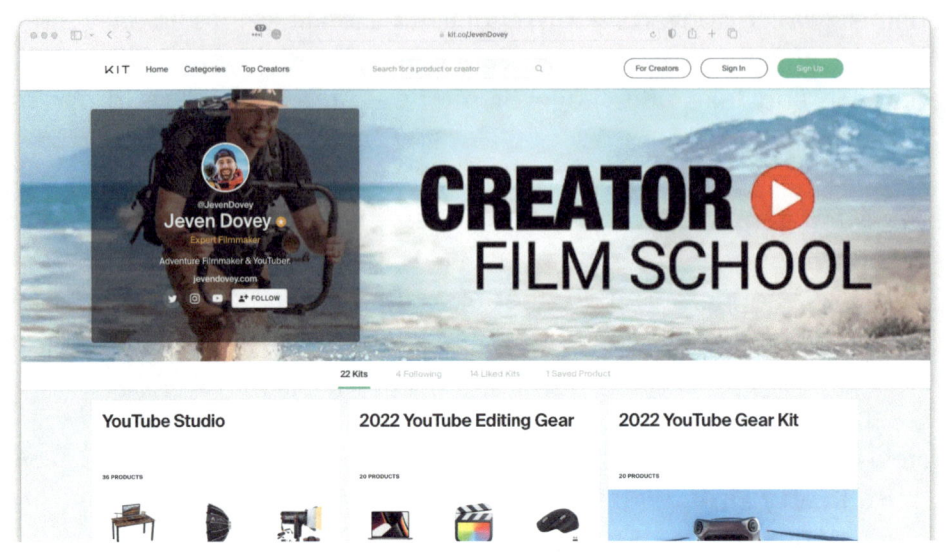

The Kit website showcases what products creators use to solve problems and use every day.

Kit can be an easier solution for making product recommendations as a lot of the messy process of finding the products to recommend, creating the affiliate links, then organizing them in a logical way, and finally making them enticing to click is managed with a clean and intuitive UI. It also includes the necessary FTC and Associates disclaimers to ensure full compliance with the program and leverages Geniuslink's technology to work for an international audience.

Kit also has tools to automatically include a link in your YouTube description to drive your audience back to your Kit profile and your product curations.

To start your adventure with Kit, you can curate lists of the books/movies/podcasts that have inspired you as a creator, the camera gear you may use, the equipment you use to record your podcast, the products you use for your morning or evening routine, or even the handful of products that you have with you everyday (commonly referred to as your "everyday carry"). Or simply use Kit to answer the next time you get the question, "What do you use for...?"

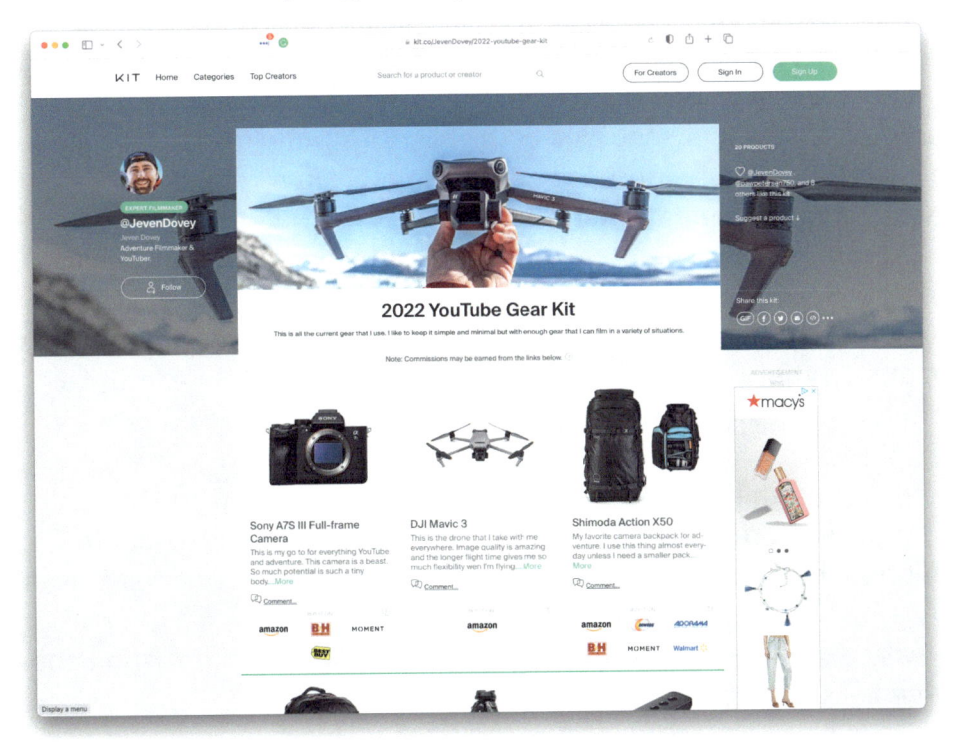

Kit natively includes FTC disclosures, international Amazon affiliate support, additional retailers to help boost conversion rates.

Again, full disclosure, we may be biased here as we at Geniuslink are now the custodians of the Kit community, but we sure do think it's a really useful tool.

Affiliate links on YouTube

An affiliate link can be placed almost anywhere (be sure to read the next chapter explaining where it is not okay to place your Amazon affiliate links) but one of the most common places we see links placed are on YouTube videos.

In the top of your video description, the text shown before the "read more" link, should include an affiliate link to any products that were shown in your video. This is easy if you are doing an unboxing or product review style video. If you are doing a vlog-style video, then any product that got a shoutout or highlight in the video should get an affiliate link in this top position. These are often referred to as your **Active Recommendations**.

In the second half of your video description, list your **Passive Recommendations,** the products that may not have gotten the top spot(s) in the video but are still relevant. This is also a good place to include any related products to those that got the top spot.

After listing the products displayed in the video, you might want to include the products that you used to create the video or that are important to you. This is often where you will see a Kit link being used.

Finally, you'll want to include any relevant disclaimer information about your links toward the bottom of the description.

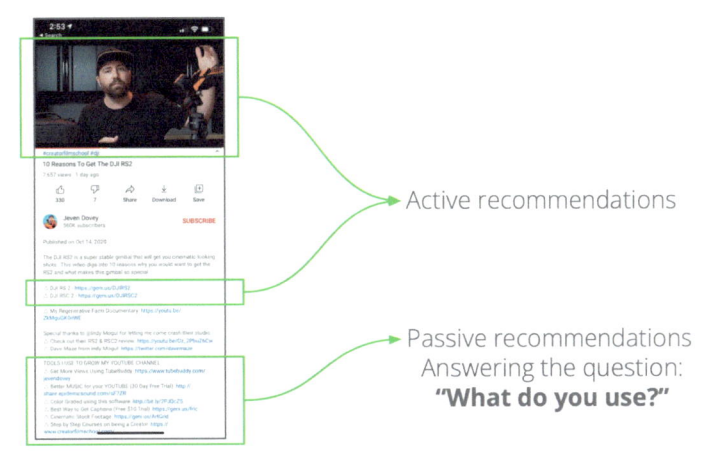

A slide from a recent presentation at a conference for YouTubers.

It's important not to get too overzealous with your affiliate links. Too many links in a video description make it look like spam and could even trigger some weirdness with the YouTube algorithm that could negatively impact your video being suggested.

With this in mind, we again recommend Kit as a tool to consolidate the affiliate links you might include in your Passive Recommendations.

One common tactic we see from new Associates is to include an Amazon affiliate link from each Amazon Associates program they are a member of for each product. We advise against this! There is a much simpler way to do this discussed in the *Going Global* chapter.

If you've adopted a multi-retailer approach to affiliate marketing (discussed further in *Advanced Amazon Affiliate Tips* chapter) then instead of including two or three different links to different retailers per product we'd strongly encourage you to take a look at Geniuslink **Choice Pages** (mobile and conversion rate optimized landing pages that can include multiple buying option for a specific product) to more elegantly accomplish the same thing.

Another tactic we've heard good results from is including an affiliate link for your Active Recommendation as the first comment on your video. Let us know how that works out for you!

A quick pro tip for those that already have a multitude of Amazon affiliate links scattered throughout their Youtube video descriptions, Geniuslink now offers a YouTube Link Optimizer[22], which can quickly replace all the amzn.to (and bhpho.to and bit.ly) links across your channel with brand new geni.us links. Imagine the time you'll save!

---

[22] https://geni.us/ytlinkoptimizer

How to Stay Compliant as an Affiliate

Understand the importance of being compliant with Amazon's Operating Agreement.

Learn the top ways to get your account in trouble.

Learn best practices for posting affiliate links on social media.

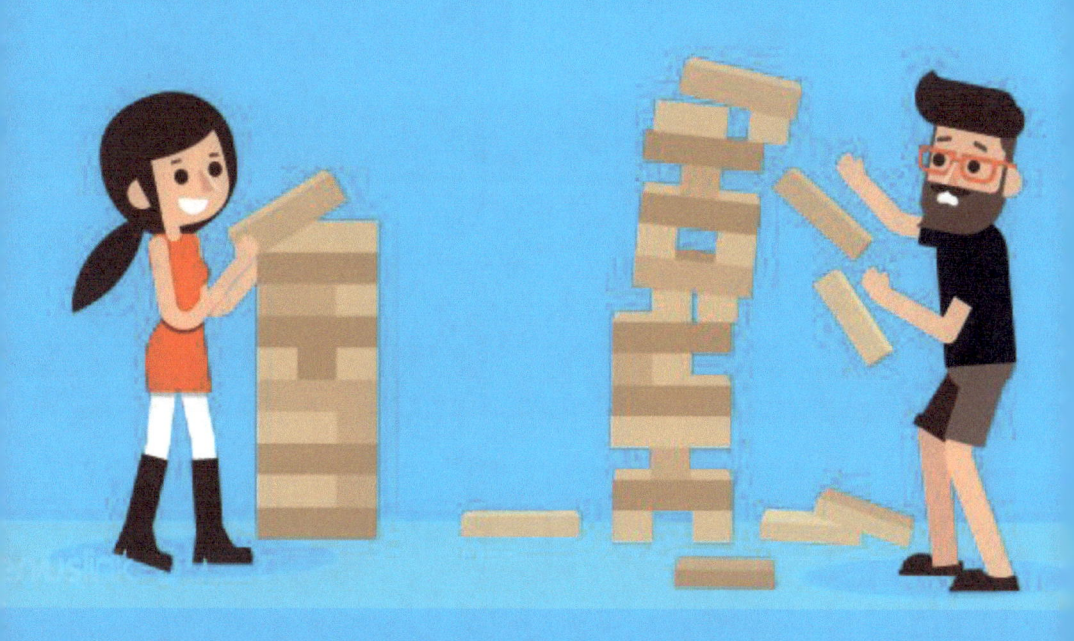

How to Stay Compliant as an Affiliate

In your excitement to get started with your new Amazon affiliate account, I'm guessing you didn't get a chance to dig into the Amazon Associates Operating Agreement[23] or the accompanying Policies[24] page, did you?

While it's not edge-of-your-seat, page-turning material, it is really important to read! The Operating Agreement and Policies outline the rules of the Amazon Associates game, and it's easy to lose the game if you don't know the rules.

For better or worse, the Amazon compliance team is really good at finding possible violations, and for affiliate publishers, pleading ignorance isn't enough to keep your account in good standing.

Further, just doing the same as other creators you see online isn't a valid excuse either. Unfortunately, there is a lot of misinformation and misunderstandings related to Amazon affiliate governance and policies, so it's best to go to the source.

We believe it's not worth risking your account with the largest affiliate program in the world due to being in a hurry, and we strongly encourage you to take the time to read the operating agreement and policies. But we want to help you get started on the right foot.

This is a topic we feel passionately about! We've written about it many times in our blog and spoken about it on stage, in webinars, and in podcast interviews.

Read More!
Guide to Getting Kicked out of Amazon Associates

---

[23] https://geni.us/amazoncomoa
[24] https://geni.us/amazoncomoapolicies

While this chapter is no substitute for reading the operating agreement and policies, we wanted to share the top reasons we've seen affiliate publishers get their accounts closed, and share a few additional notes for those who plan to primarily use social media for their affiliate marketing campaigns. Please don't make these same mistakes!

Obligatory disclaimer before we proceed: we are not a legal authority on this topic and any actions taken as a result of reading this section should be done with the knowledge that the reader is doing so of their own accord, and they may want to consult their own legal counsel when in doubt. This book is also a static accounting of the rules, which may change with little or no notice. Refer to the Amazon operating agreement and policies before deciding on a strategy.

Cloaking links

This is a broad category, and there are really three different things that can get you in trouble here if you don't pay attention.

No cloaking

Cloaking, in the world of affiliate marketing, is the process of intentionally hiding or disguising that a link is actually an affiliate link. This is a practice you absolutely want to avoid with your Amazon affiliate links.

Inside the Amazon Associates Operating Agreement, on the Policies page, in section 6. "Content on Your Site," it states (emphasis is our own):

*(v) **You will not cloak, hide, spoof, or otherwise obscure the URL** of your Site containing Special Links (including by use of Redirecting Links) or the user agent of the application in which Program Content is displayed or used such that we cannot reasonably determine the site or application from which a customer clicks through such Special Link to the Amazon Site.*

While this is about as clear as mud, we read the above as Amazon doesn't want you to intentionally hide your site from them.

It's also important to clarify that link shortening is not cloaking unless the intention is to hide the referrer (and or user agent) which some, very specific link shorteners provide. By default most link shorteners, including Geniuslink, redirect with a "301" or "302" which preserves the referrer, user agent, etc. and thus ensures compliance with this policy.

Redirects and Link Shorteners are okay

There is often a lot of confusion around if it's okay to use a link shortener (short answer is "yes it is!") and that is typically due to the subsequent section of the Operating Agreement Policies also being written in a confusing way.

Section 6. "Content on Your Site," reads (again emphasis our own):

*(w) **You will not use a link shortening service**, button, hyperlink or other ad placement in a manner **that makes it unclear that you are linking to an Amazon Site**.*

The second part of the sentence brings it all together: make it clear you are linking to Amazon.

How to Stay Compliant as an Affiliate

It's absolutely okay to use a link shortener with your Amazon affiliate links. However, when doing so, it's key that you disclose the destination of your link, which leads us to the next consideration.

Always mentioning Amazon

Shopper Trust is an important theme to Amazon and that relates to their affiliate program as well. When you post Amazon affiliate links using a third-party tool, like Geniuslink, it's really important that you mention "Amazon" in near proximity to the link. This is especially important for shortened links used on social media. It's essential the shopper knows where they are going when they click on that link. Doing this can also help with conversion rates by helping the shopper better trust the link.

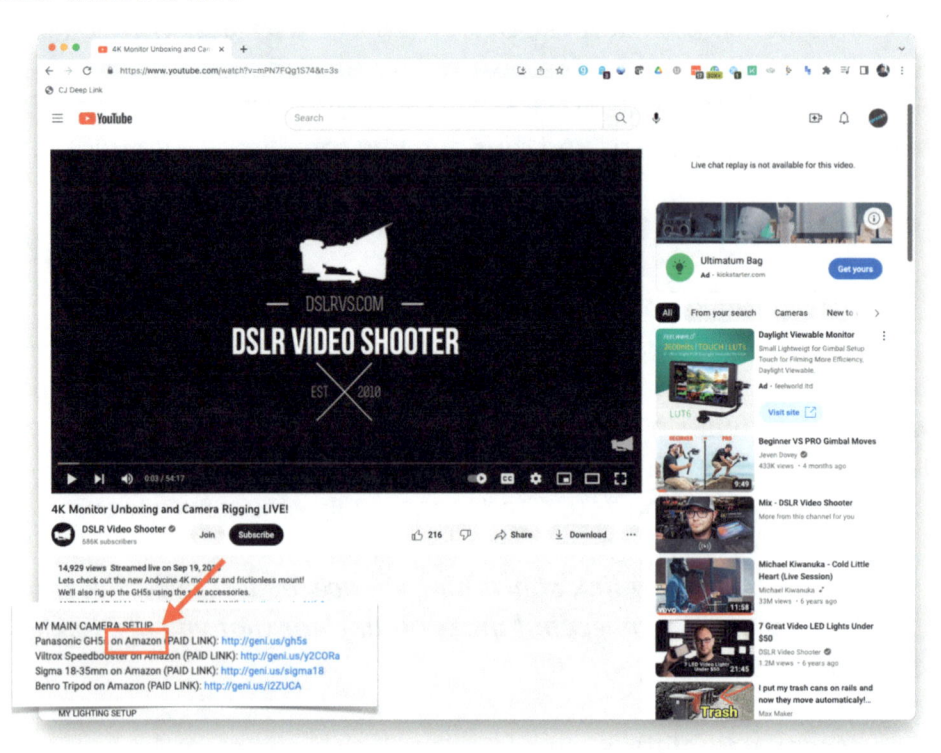

Notice the "on Amazon" mentioned before the geni.us link to ensure the reader knows where they are being sent.

When your affiliate link is live on a website, it's important the consumer knows where the link will take them. You can include visual cues in near proximity of the links, or include "Amazon" in the call to action. Further, some third-party tools let the link remain an Amazon link, so when the shopper mouses over the link in their browser, the status bar shows the Amazon URL.

Listing all your sites (and social media channels)

Remember that step when you were signing up for the Amazon affiliate program where you listed the various sites and social media channels you were planning on using your links? Well, have you kept that updated?

It's easy to have a shifting strategy, place your affiliate links in new places, and forget to update that list via the Associates Central dashboard.

Having affiliate links posted somewhere that's not listed in your account can get you in trouble with the Amazon compliance team, so we recommend getting into a regular monthly habit to ensure everything is up to date on your site list.

Note: if you are taking advantage of Geniuslink Choice Pages, or any other landing page service for that matter, you'll also want to include "geni.us," or the service's domain that you use, in your website list.

How to Stay Compliant as an Affiliate

Home › Your Associates Account › **Edit Your Website, Mobile App, And Alexa Skill List**

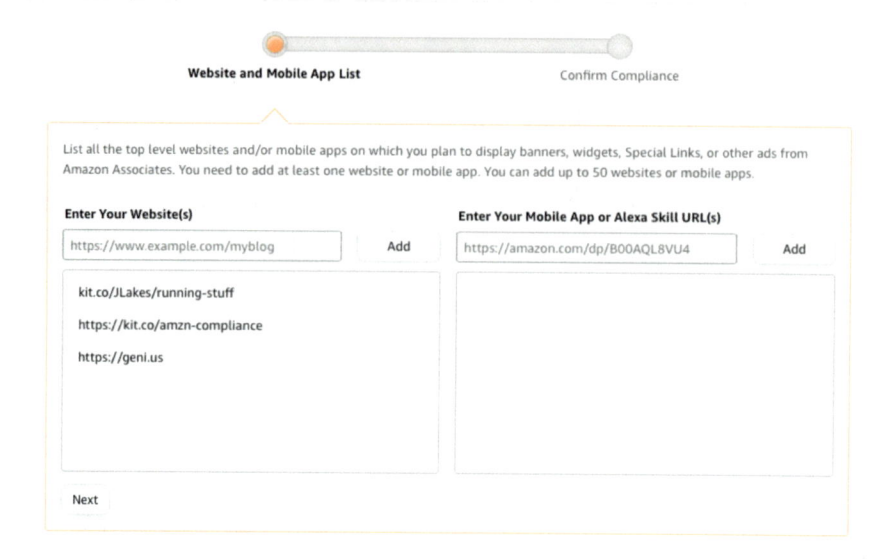

Website and Mobile App List — Confirm Compliance

List all the top level websites and/or mobile apps on which you plan to display banners, widgets, Special Links, or other ads from Amazon Associates. You need to add at least one website or mobile app. You can add up to 50 websites or mobile apps.

Enter Your Website(s)

https://www.example.com/myblog   Add

- kit.co/JLakes/running-stuff
- https://kit.co/amzn-compliance
- https://geni.us

Enter Your Mobile App or Alexa Skill URL(s)

https://amazon.com/dp/B00AQL8VU4   Add

Next

Your Site List inside Amazon Associates Central should be kept to date and include all of the places you share your Amazon affiliate links.

Offline links

As mentioned in the first point about cloaking, Amazon doesn't like it when they can't track or review the placement of your affiliate links and as such has a rule about no "offline" placements.

Ultimately, this means **affiliate links aren't allowed to be directly placed into an email, PDFs, eBooks, in print, QR codes, etc.**

Essentially any place where the Associates compliance team is unable to review and confirm the placement of affiliate links and therefore, the shopper experience, is off limits. It's imperative that the compliance team is able to confirm an affiliate publisher isn't doing anything deceptive to get shoppers into Amazon.

You may have come across an affiliate link in an email newsletter before, but unless you've been given explicit permission from Amazon it's technically against their rules to do this.

How to Stay Compliant as an Affiliate

However, there is a legitimate workaround for when you want to place an affiliate link in an email, PDF, ebook, printed, or via a QR code -- instead of using a direct Amazon affiliate link, **place a link to a Geniuslink "Choice Page."**

These Choice Pages[25] are optimized landing pages that are specifically built to recommend a product via an affiliate link and include the necessary disclaimer. Because the affiliate link technically lives on this landing page, it's not in violation of the Associates Operating Agreement. Learn more about Choice Pages in the *Advanced Amazon Affiliate Tips* chapter - Advanced Amazon Affiliate Tips.

---

[25] https://geni.us/choicepages

How to Stay Compliant as an Affiliate

A Choice Page promotes a specific product with one or more retailer's affiliate links included below.

It's important to note that by using Choice Pages, you also need to update your list of websites and social media channels where your affiliate links go so you aren't labeled as cloaking your links as described above.

Mentioning prices (or availability)

It's important to note that Amazon's product catalog is constantly updating. Since Amazon is fastidious about maintaining "shopper trust" you can quickly see why Amazon doesn't like it when you mention specific pricing or availability of a product -- it's likely that shortly after you publish this information it will be out of date and wrong.

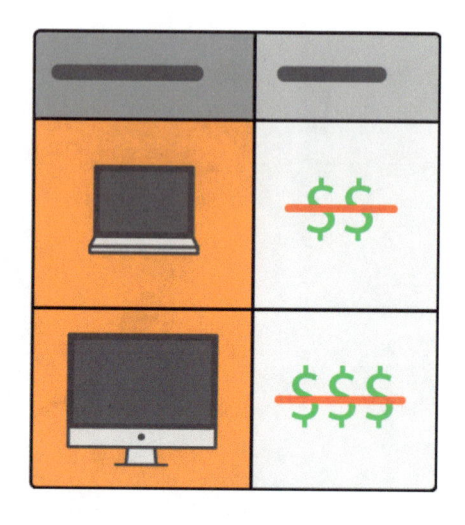

As a result, Amazon has a hard rule that any mention of pricing or availability can't be more than 24 hours old and strongly recommends that if you plan to use pricing or availability in your affiliate marketing, you take advantage of a tool that leverages the Product Advertising API or use it directly yourself to ensure your pricing and availability is as up to date as possible.

Using star ratings and reviews

Similar to the note above, due to the volatility of their store, Amazon doesn't like affiliate publishers using "static" versions of their star ratings or product reviews. These are available to use if you are using a "dynamic" source, specifically Amazon's PA API or a tool that takes advantage of it.

They do not appear to have any problem with you using your own rating system or your own reviews! Just be sure to make it clear that it's yours.

Asking for a click (or bookmark) on your affiliate link

Don't do it!

Amazon doesn't allow any sort of "incentivized" behavior concerning the promotion of their affiliate links. Violating this rule can be as simple as mentioning your page or channel is "supported" or "sponsored" by Amazon's affiliate program.

Additionally, asking someone to click your affiliate link before making a purchase on Amazon or asking someone to bookmark your affiliate link for future purchases will certainly land you in hot water with Amazon when you are caught.

Link to products or services

Don't use affiliate links for sending people to support articles or other areas on Amazon's site where something isn't specifically for sale.

Amazon's affiliate program is there to reward you for helping them sell more products and services. It's there so you can add value to the buying process.

As a result, you can quickly get kicked out of the affiliate program by pointing your affiliate links to support articles on Amazon.

One of our favorite stories illustrating this point is of someone getting their Associates account shut down when they wrote a detailed article on how to do a return with Amazon. The article was great and they were able to get it ranking fairly well on the search engines and capture some sizable traffic. But unfortunately they created an affiliate link that pointed to the page on Amazon used to initiate a return.

While they were initially earning a lot of commissions they were soon caught and all those commissions plus everything they were earning from legitimate ways was clawed back and their account was permanently closed. Definitely a bummer but a great lesson for the rest of us.

Not including an affiliate disclaimer

Related to calling out the destination of your link when you use a link management tool, letting your audience know that you are promoting a product and that money is on the line is absolutely critical in the world of affiliate marketing, especially with the Amazon affiliate program. Notice the "Paid Link" right next to the "on Amazon" disclosure from the example we used earlier.

How to Stay Compliant as an Affiliate

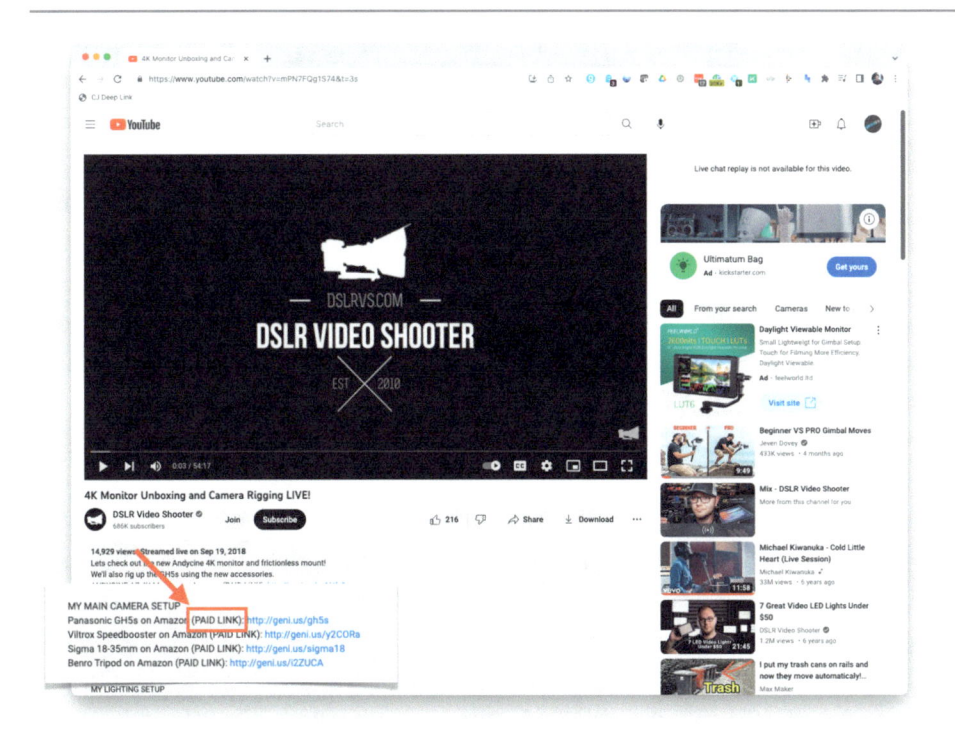

Notice the "(PAID LINK)" mentioned before the affiliate link ensures the reader knows there is a commercial interest with this link.

There are actually two levels at which it's important to make disclosures and publicly state your usage of any affiliate program, and for Amazon's program in particular.
- One is at the "link level" to fulfill the FTC guidelines
- Another is at the site or channel level to ensure compliance with the Amazon Associates Operating Agreement.

1/ FTC disclaimer

The Federal Trade Commission has the mandate to help ensure transparency to the American shopper, specifically that they know when they are being advertised to. In the eyes of the FTC, being "advertised to" includes using affiliate links when you recommend products. As a result, to be in good standing, you need to make a disclosure that is "clear" and "conspicuous."

While we aren't qualified to say exactly what this means (and strongly encourage you to consult with your own legal counsel!), from our own understanding saying "affiliate link" isn't good enough. The FTC argues that "affiliate" isn't a term the average consumer knows. Because of this, we recommend making sure your disclosure includes verbiage about "earning" money. Referencing the prior screenshot "Paid Link" works well here though we also regularly see "#ad" or "#CommissionsEarned".

A disclaimer in the footer of your site doesn't fit the FTC guidelines either. Rather, the disclaimer should be in near proximity to your links or at the beginning of your article in full view.

These rules also apply to social media, not just websites! Be sure to include your FTC link-level disclaimers in your tweets, posts, and video descriptions - anywhere you might place your affiliate link. If you don't have room or don't like the look, then you may want to check out Choice Pages which include a built-in FTC disclosure.

2/ Amazon Associates disclaimer

In addition to the FTC disclaimer, the Associates program also requires you to include a notice to your community in regards to your relationship with Amazon.

Read More!
Amazon Compliance - An FTC Reminder (blog)

This disclosure has been shortened to a single sentence that simply reads:

"As an Amazon Associate I earn from qualifying purchases."

Unlike the FTC disclosure, this one is allowed to be included in pages that speak to your site more broadly, such as your "Terms of Service" or "About Us" page.

For social media, the Amazon disclosure can live in the "Info" or "About" section of your social media profile.

Additional concerns for social media

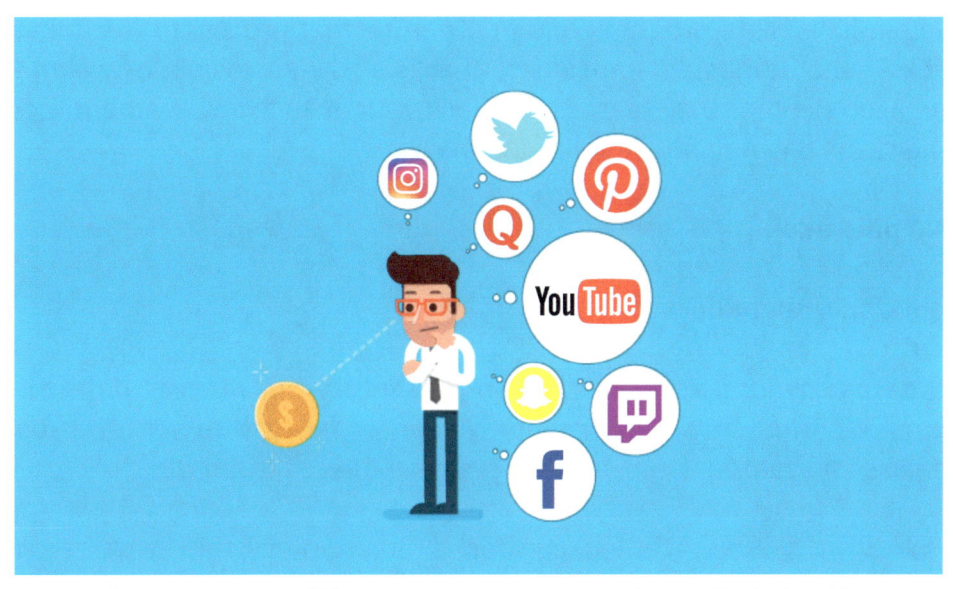

Using the Amazon affiliate program on Twitter, Twitch, Pinterest, YouTube, Facebook, and other social media platforms is growing quickly and is fully supported by Amazon, with a few caveats. They've outlined a few clarifications for social media use in a separate article[26] In short, those include:

---

[26] https://geni.us/amznsocialmedia

Only in your channel

The Amazon affiliate program makes the requirement that you only post links when "You are the sole moderator of the account that you plan to post to." This means that posting your affiliate links in forums, groups, or in replies/comments is a violation of the Amazon TOS.

Public

Your posts with affiliate links must be made public.

Amazon has a comprehensive review process to ensure compliance within its affiliate program, and in order for that process to work, your links must be posted somewhere that is easily accessible by them. If Amazon's compliance team can't check your links to review them then they can't ensure you are following the rules.

No paid ads

Amazon straight up says:

"No, you cannot use affiliate links in paid ads or pay ("boost") posts that include affiliate links. They cannot contain or be used to advertise your Amazon affiliate links and send the customer directly to Amazon."

However, if you are looking for a solution to this, we'd again recommend linking from your ads to a Choice Page, or an optimized landing page. From there you can include an affiliate link.

Gray areas in the Operating Agreement

While the Operating Agreement and Policies page answers numerous questions and clarifies a lot of things, you'll still find there are gray areas. When you come across these, and they are applicable to what you are trying to do, it's best **not to ignore them** and assume you can make a good argument should it ever become an issue (trust me, they play *their* game by *their* rules).

As a result, we recommend these two things:

First, think about the situation from Amazon's perspective and be honest with yourself. Would Amazon want you to do this? The likely answer is probably no.

Second, ask them! There are multiple ways to contact Amazon affiliate support including by chat, a phone number, and a form to start an email thread[27].

However, when you ask a question, we recommend you don't just ask once but ask many times via different channels and different mediums.

We'd encourage you to ask that same question, phrased slightly differently, at least three times. Compare the responses, and use the response that came up most often.

Be sure to record those conversations somewhere in case something does go sideways so you can point back to them. This may get you some leniency, but don't bank on it!

---

[27] https://geni.us/associatescontact

How to Stay Compliant as an Affiliate

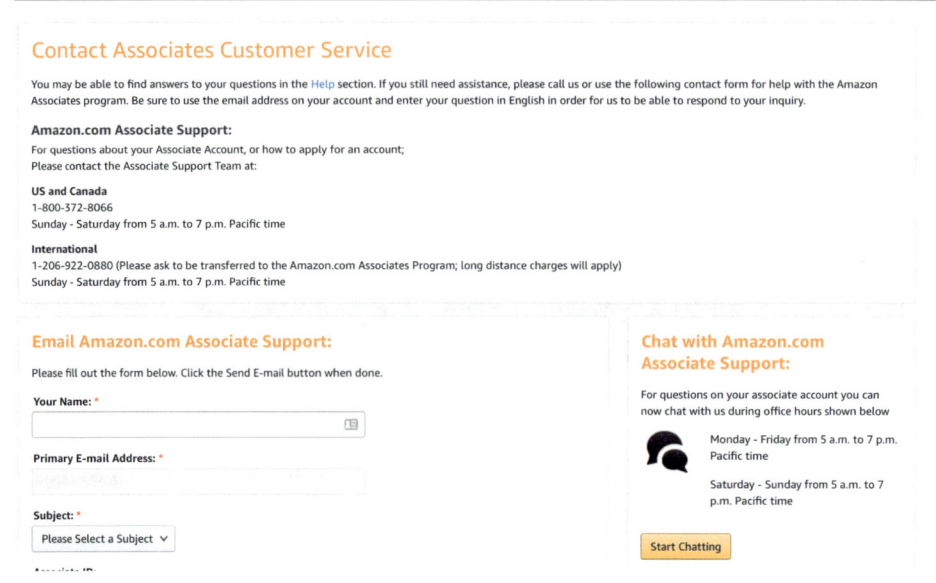

Contact Associates Customer Service

You may be able to find answers to your questions in the Help section. If you still need assistance, please call us or use the following contact form for help with the Amazon Associates program. Be sure to use the email address on your account and enter your question in English in order for us to be able to respond to your inquiry.

Amazon.com Associate Support:
For questions about your Associate Account, or how to apply for an account;
Please contact the Associate Support Team at:

US and Canada
1-800-372-8066
Sunday - Saturday from 5 a.m. to 7 p.m. Pacific time

International
1-206-922-0880 (Please ask to be transferred to the Amazon.com Associates Program; long distance charges will apply)
Sunday - Saturday from 5 a.m. to 7 p.m. Pacific time

Email Amazon.com Associate Support:

Please fill out the form below. Click the Send E-mail button when done.

Your Name: *

Primary E-mail Address: *

Subject: *

Please Select a Subject

Chat with Amazon.com Associate Support:

For questions on your associate account you can now chat with us during office hours shown below

Monday - Friday from 5 a.m. to 7 p.m. Pacific time

Saturday - Sunday from 5 a.m. to 7 p.m. Pacific time

Start Chatting

Amazon Associates has multiple ways you can contact them, just be sure if you are asking an important question to ask it a few different times in a few different ways to ensure you get a consistent response.

How to Increase Your Commissions (aka Best Practices)

Learn how SEO is crucial to success with affiliate marketing.

See how Conversion Rate Optimization is also an essential skill.

Read how building an audience should be your top priority.

From supporting tens of thousands of Amazon affiliates over the years, we are in the unique position of having some really interesting conversations with bloggers, creators, and influencers who use the program. We've also learned, for the most part, there is no "silver bullet," and big monthly affiliate payouts come from months, and years, of hard work.

We've also learned the "short cuts" are typically just slow death sentences to getting removed from the program. Doing things the right way is critical to long-term health and wealth with your affiliate marketing efforts.

We have also heard strategies and tactics that get repeated time and time again which lead to a successful business centered around affiliate marketing. We have aggregated those below so you have some best practices to get started.

Please note: what works well for one person may not work well for you, so don't be afraid of being agile and tweaking these techniques or adding others, to build your own personal playbook for maximizing your affiliate commissions.

Search Engine Optimization

While not specific to affiliate marketing, SEO is the backbone of internet marketing. Whether you have a YouTube channel or a niche authority blog, or both, it's important you drive people who have a general interest in your niche to your content so they can click on your affiliate links. So while you hone your affiliate marketing skills, be sure to at least dabble in SEO skills as well.

While SEO is not our specialty, there are some amazing people, who also happen to be affiliate marketers, who offer great resources.

How to Increase Your Commissions (aka Best Practices)

Two of our favorites are **Doug Cunnington from Niche Site Project** (nichesiteproject.com) and **Spencer Haws from Niche Pursuits** (nichepursuits.com).

Outside of the general platitudes of building backlinks and doing keyword research, there are a few tidbits we've heard repeated from people we trust.

First is a focus on **internal links** -- the links from one of your pages to another page, or from one video to another in your YouTube channel. Oftentimes internal links are an afterthought. However, many are finding that optimization of your website around internal links can be a higher ROI than building backlinks, especially for a more mature site.

Internal Links

Link high value keywords on your website to important pages on your site.

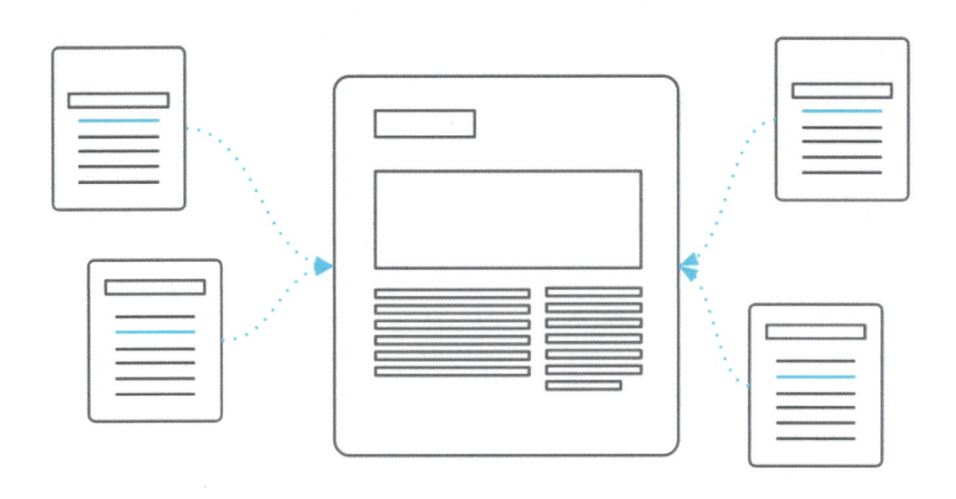

For larger or more mature sites, a concentrated effort in internal linking can yield significant SEO gains.

A few additional resources for learning more about best practices include:

- **Geniuslink Blog**: *Best Practices for Using Internal Links on Your Amazon Affiliate Site* (https://geni.us/blog-InternalLinks)

- **ShoutMeLoud**: *How To Build Internal Links for SEO in WordPress* (https://geni.us/SML-InternalLinks)

- **LinkWhisper**: WordPress plugin to automate internal links (https://geni.us/LinkWhisper)

Next is to **niche down** and not only focus your site or channel on very specific areas but follow the same principle with your keyword research. It seems that focusing on long-tail keywords with low competition will often yield promising results well before mid-body or top keywords, keywords with more competition. Winning lots of little battles for traffic is not only good for generating traffic, and subsequently affiliate commissions, but is helpful for morale too!

A focus on **Buyer's keywords** can also be helpful in getting the right traffic to your site or channel. This means targeting people who may be lower in the marketing funnel and who are more mentally prepared to make the purchase than those who are just starting their research. While there is a whole art and science to it, riffing off of keywords like "[product-name] comparison" or "What kind of [product-name] should I get?" will help you narrow in on buyers that are more ready to actually make a purchase.

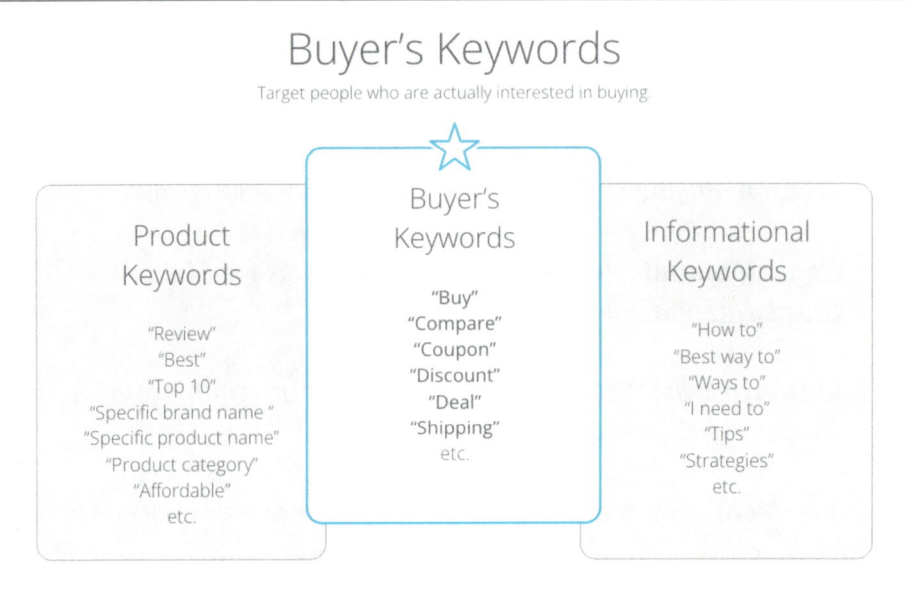

How to Increase Your Commissions (aka Best Practices)

Buyer's Keywords
Target people who are actually interested in buying.

Product Keywords
"Review"
"Best"
"Top 10"
"Specific brand name"
"Specific product name"
"Product category"
"Affordable"
etc.

Buyer's Keywords
"Buy"
"Compare"
"Coupon"
"Discount"
"Deal"
"Shipping"
etc.

Informational Keywords
"How to"
"Best way to"
"Ways to"
"I need to"
"Tips"
"Strategies"
etc.

When combining affiliate marketing with SEO it's important to target the right keywords that will lead to a sale and not just research.

A good additional resource here is Backlinko's Keyword Commercial Intent article (https://geni.us/CommercialIntent).

Multiple affiliate links

An easy trap to fall into early in your affiliate journey is to write a good product review but then only include a single affiliate link at the end of your article. This limits you to a single chance to get a click and earn a commission.

How to Increase Your Commissions (aka Best Practices)

Placement
Don't use just one affiliate link!

A well done article should include multiple affiliate links, not just one at the end.

The best practice is to actually include multiple affiliate links for the product throughout the page.
- Include a link as early as the first paragraph.
- Include a link when you mention the name of the specific product you are reviewing.
- Pictures of the product are also good places to include the affiliate link.
- Including a call to action halfway through your review can also be helpful.

- Finish the article with a strong call to action and an affiliate link.

Balance is the key here. Going overboard with the affiliate links comes off as spammy and can actually lower the trust the reader has in your review.

Related Products

Another way to include additional affiliate links on your page is by including a section in your review about products related to the one you are reviewing. You see Amazon doing this all of the time with their "Customers Who Bought This Item Also Bought" section on every product page. It's a great practice and something you can easily apply to your review articles and still add value to the buying process.

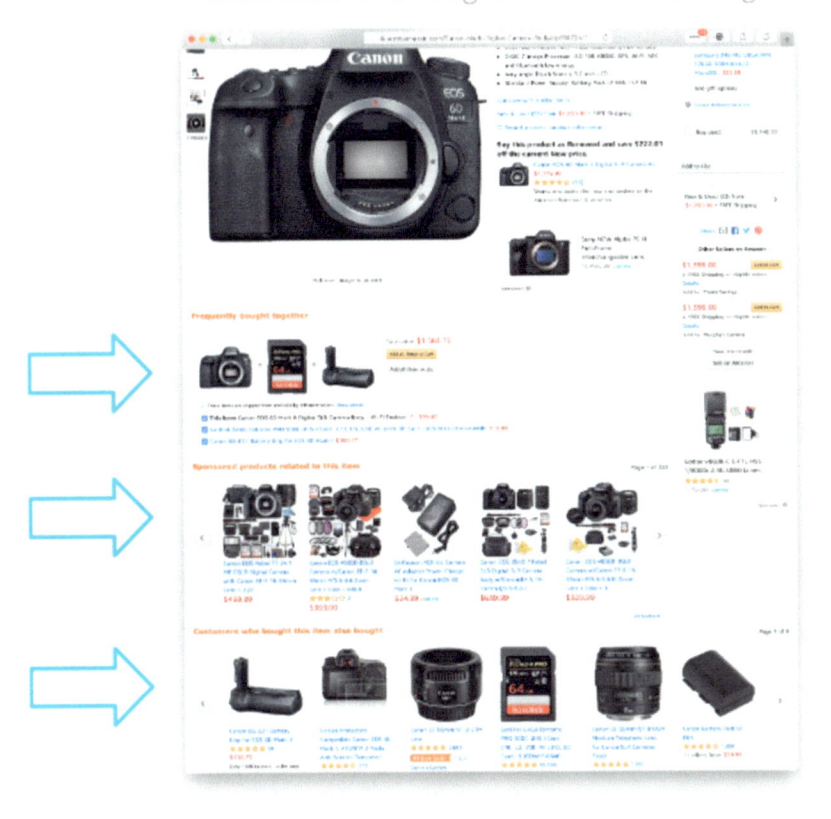

How to Increase Your Commissions (aka Best Practices)

Amazon loves to call out related products to help increase shopping cart sizes.

For YouTubers, a tool like Kit.co where you can curate products that work well together is a great way to recommend related products.

Call-to-action

A **CTA** (**Call-to-action**) is a phrase you use to encourage your readers to take action, click on your affiliate link, and move through the buying process. Experimenting with your CTAs can lead to an incremental

How to Increase Your Commissions (aka Best Practices)

increase in conversion rates, but it's something you also need to be careful with!

Having a strong call to action can be helpful in the conversion from page visits to link clicks. For example, ending your CTA with the word "now" to inspire action in a timely manner.

You'll also want to try and include a CTA in the browser window before you start to scroll, and in the first paragraph, which allows those in your audience who are eager to buy an easy excuse to move forward with one of your affiliate links.

Call-To-Action
Experiment to find what's best

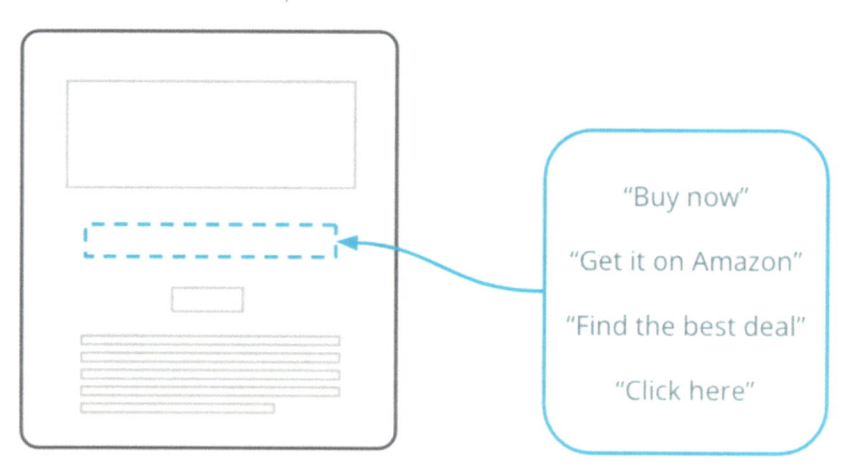

"Buy now"

"Get it on Amazon"

"Find the best deal"

"Click here"

How you encourage a buyer to move forward is incredibly important in making the sale.

It's important to remember not to get too aggressive with your CTAs and be cautious of the Amazon affiliate rules. This primarily means being cognizant of "incentivizing" clicks as we talked about in the prior section. Further, you want to be wary of what are referred to as **weasel**

words (such as "discount, lowest, sale, etc.") that may not actually be true of the product being sold at Amazon, at least at that specific time. Note that weasel words in SEO are encouraged, just not in your CTAs.

Including multiple CTAs through your page can be helpful -- just be sure you don't overdo it and sound too much like a used car salesman.

For **YouTubers** in particular, don't forget that **you aren't allowed to ask for a click from your audience.** This is a great way to get your Amazon Associates account closed.

Comparisons

A very common practice these days is around reviewing multiple competing products in a single page or video, along the lines of a "buying guide." This allows for a few different best practices to peek through, including using comparison tables, being authentic, and anchoring.

Comparison tables are another tool that Amazon uses regularly on their site. Keep scrolling past the "Customers Who Bought This Item Also Bought" section and you are likely to come across one. These tables are great to start off with an affiliate link behind a strong CTA and a good way to recap the aspects of the products you were reviewing.

How to Increase Your Commissions (aka Best Practices)

Comparison Tables
Cast a wider net and ensure your content resonates

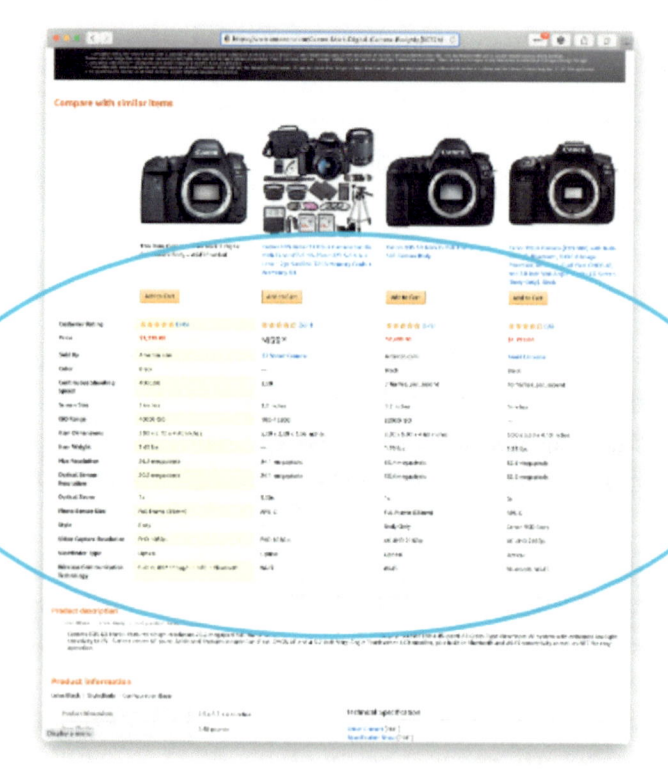

Amazon is a huge fan of comparison tables. You should be too!

Authenticity is a very important aspect of doing product reviews and something we strongly recommend. You'll likely find that when you give realistic reviews and don't skip over the negatives of a product, you'll find your conversion rates increase as people are more willing to trust you. With any product review, a section that highlights the not-so-great aspects is important. Affiliate marketers often find it's easier to be critical of a product when comparing it to its peers as it often feels more natural.

Finally, comparisons are a great place to introduce the concept of **anchoring**. Anchoring is a "cognitive bias" that you likely see a hundred times a day but subconsciously ignore. It is the practice of how you order things, so that you place the item you don't intend to sell first, making the second or third item seem more favorable. For example, placing the most expensive product first makes the second, a lower-price item, seem more attractive instead of ordering the list from least expensive to most expensive.

One thing to note is that including too many products in your comparisons can lead to the paradox of choice and actually hamper the buying process. Three to five products are the sweet spot.

Building a community

Typically when we start out in our affiliate marketing journey, we are eager to make recommendations and generate revenue. While this is certainly an important goal, it's important not to be short-sighted.

Many experts in the world of affiliate marketing actually prioritize generating affiliate sales as a secondary goal. Their primary goal is to build an engaged and active community, which doesn't sound so different from the life of a YouTuber or social media influencer, right? It's only after having built an audience of some size (1K subscribers is a great start!) that they start to make product recommendations and generate affiliate revenue. Once you have a community and have built trust, you'll find that making recommendations of products and services (via affiliate links) is significantly easier and your campaigns will convert much higher.

Prioritize Engagement
Sell yourself, build trust, then recommend products

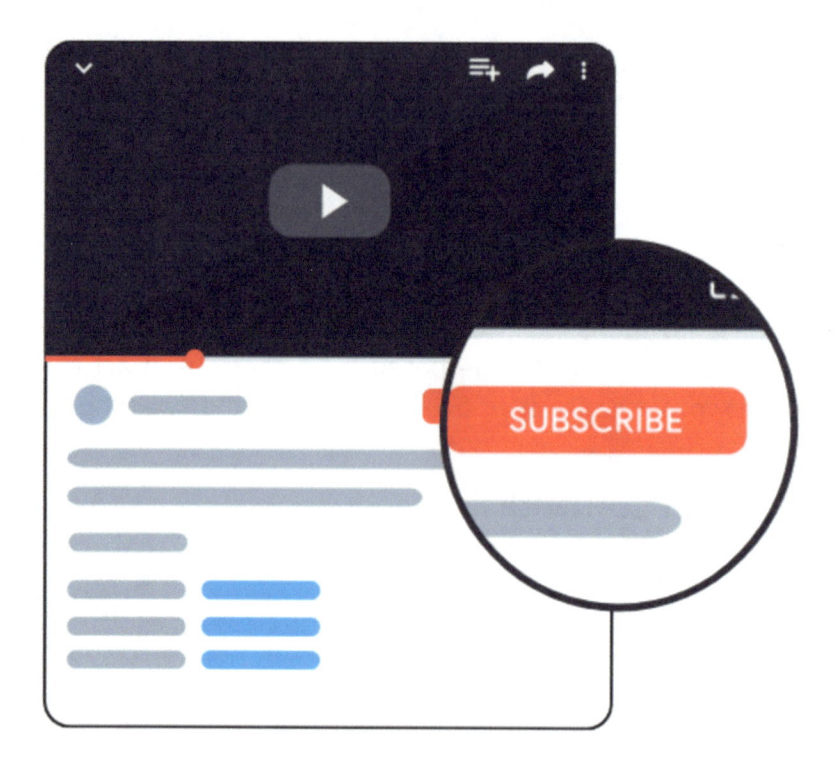

Build an engaged audience first, then recommend products and services.

For some channels, this is easier than others. For example, on YouTube, a primary goal is to build that subscriber base. Those subscribers are the community, and once you have a large active group, it's easier to make recommendations that result in sales.

For websites, this can be a bit more of a challenge as that "community" aspect isn't as built-in as it is with social media. As a result, a primary goal for niche websites is to build an email list and then keep that active with regular emails. The website eventually becomes less important and the email list, aka the community, becomes much more important.

Build An Email List
The one channel you fully own, everything else is rented.

At the end of the day, a good email list can be your biggest asset.

Just remember, you can't embed Amazon affiliate links directly into your emails! But you can use your emails to drive them to a landing page (or Choice Page) from where you have your Amazon affiliate links.

International shoppers

The internet has never been more global, and chances are the people visiting your site, reading your posts, and watching your videos are from all over the world. One of the most amazing things about the internet is how it brings together people who care about super-specific and niche things into tribes no matter where they are from. It's also easy to forget about the international aspect of your audience, but it's something we strongly recommend you check on, especially after you've started to see some initial traction with your site or channel.

While at some point you might consider localizing your page or channel with additional languages, if someone is visiting your site or channel now, the language isn't necessarily the biggest hurdle for them.

We have found that reading or consuming content in a foreign language is way easier than buying something from a foreign store!

Put yourself in their shoes -- there is often no harm in reading something in a foreign language. Worst part is you misunderstand bits here and there or you don't completely follow along. However, trying to buy something in a foreign storefront can quickly lead to wasted time and costly mistakes like:

- Buying the wrong product,
- Credit card fees for a foreign currency transaction
- Need to set up a new account
- Expensive and slow shipping, Or even worse, realizing after everything that they won't even ship to your country

How to Increase Your Commissions (aka Best Practices)

Amazon knows this and has spent billions of dollars on a solution. Amazon currently has 22 independent storefronts around the world[28] and continues to launch new Amazon storefronts in various parts of the world to cater to shoppers in specific countries and regions. When Amazon does this, they can offer a shopping experience in a local language in local currency with fast and efficient shipping and delivery, as well as the appropriate taxes. Ultimately, this is a much more streamlined buying experience and results in much higher conversion rates.

So while it is possible to send your whole audience to a single Amazon store, and earn some affiliate commissions, if you are like the thousands of clients we have at Geniuslink, you'll likely see a significant increase in your conversion rates and commissions when you start sending each of your foreign shoppers to the appropriate product in their local Amazon storefront. More about how to optimize your Amazon affiliate links for your global audience is in the next section.

---

[28] See Appendix A

Going Global With Your Affiliate Links

Understand how Amazon's affiliate program is geographically fragmented.

Explore how your revenue may be impacted by "geo-fragmentation."

Learn best practices, and tools, for supporting and monetizing an international audience.

Going Global With Your Affiliate Links

As we alluded to in the prior chapter, one of the key optimizations is to expand past using a single Amazon affiliate program and move to use many of the regional affiliate programs concurrently.

Traditionally, Amazon links are static and send everyone, no matter where they are from, to the same destination. So there is some work involved in getting past this, but working through the setup has two major benefits.

First, and most importantly, you can improve user experience for your international community. By sending them to the correct product but in their local Amazon storefront, they can take advantage of their Prime membership, can transact in their local currency, should receive the product faster via local shipping, and having the process in their native language should reduce the friction in the whole buying process. This improvement in the buying experience should increase your revenue and grow your international audience.

Please note, however, that just signing up for an international Amazon affiliate program won't magically make your links work (more on that in a minute).

The second major benefit is financial. By moving to an "intelligent" Amazon affiliate link, one that sends foreign shoppers to the right product in their local Amazon storefront, you should also see an increase in your conversion rates, your earnings per click, and your total revenue.

This happens because the international shoppers who you were sending to your local storefront, like your UK shoppers getting sent to Amazon.com, had a significantly lower chance of converting. However, by sending your UK shoppers to the correct product in Amazon.co.uk, the Amazon storefront specifically optimized to support shoppers in the UK, you'll see a much higher conversion rate.

A link management tool that supports geo-targeting, like Geniuslink, can help ensure your international audience is sent to the right product in their local Amazon store and that your efforts are rewarded by now collecting international commissions.

It's important to note that not every visitor to your site, or click on your affiliate link, will come from one of the countries that has a native Amazon storefront. That's okay, most Amazon affiliate link localization tools have some "nearest neighbor" or intelligence to send shoppers to the storefront that is most optimized for them.

It's also worth noting that not all products are available in all the Amazon storefronts. A good Amazon Associates link management tool will default to the best buying experience instead of sending a shopper to the wrong product or on a wild goose chase.

Is your audience international?

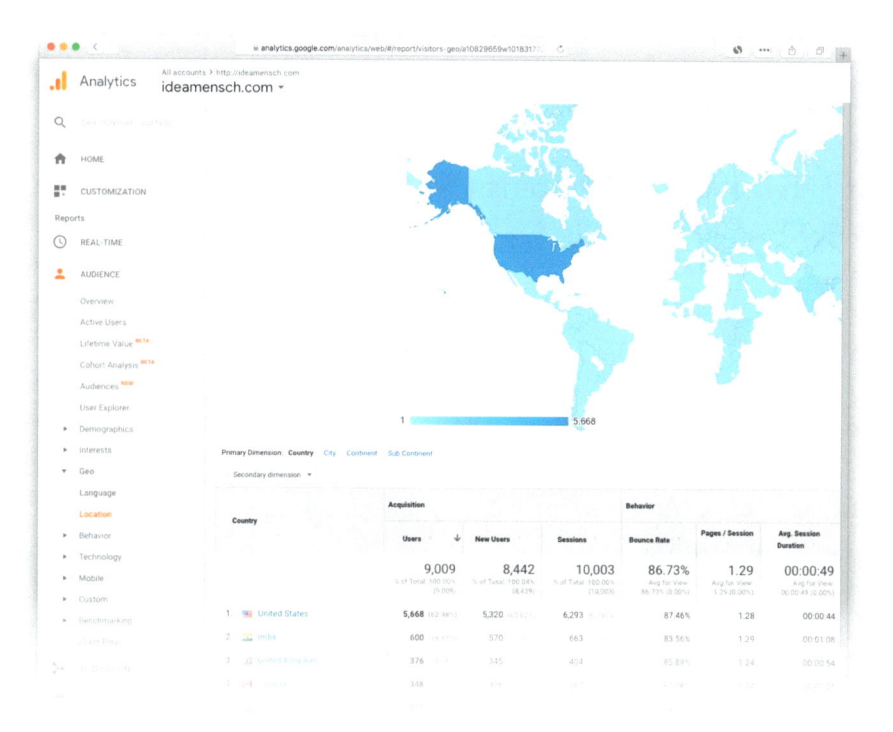

Google Analytics is one way to see how diverse your traffic might be if you run a website.

Many of us don't realize how diverse our audience is after spending all of our time in the weeds creating content, working on SEO, building affiliate links, etc. As a result, I would encourage you to take a moment right now and check your site or channel analytics.

Most every content management system I've ever seen has some sort of analytics package with geographic breakdown, and I encourage you to find and review that right now.

As you look at your analytics, you have two questions to answer:

1. How much of my traffic is domestic and matches the Amazon store and affiliate program I'm currently using?
2. How much of my traffic is international? And more specifically, what are my top five international countries?

If your international audience is less than 10% of your total, then I'd encourage you to just jump to the next section, but don't lose sight of this stat. Keep checking your geographic breakdown regularly, and once 10% of your audience is coming from international countries come back to this chapter.

If international traffic is more than 10%, then please keep reading. We've found that for every 10% of international traffic you get when you localize your Amazon affiliate links you'll see your total revenue increase by about 5%[29].

If your site or channel had 50% international traffic and you were making $1K a month from Amazon.com commissions, then localizing your Amazon affiliate links should add another $250 to your total revenue. This brings you up to $1,250 a month in commissions with no additional work or traffic. This $250 is essentially "found money" or money that was previously just "left on the table!"

International Amazon affiliate programs

As of this writing, there are now 20 public Amazon affiliate programs and two private programs spread across the world. In the past, we have seen new Amazon storefronts and their corresponding affiliate programs launching approximately every six to 12 months.

---

[29] https://geni.us/amznimprovedroi

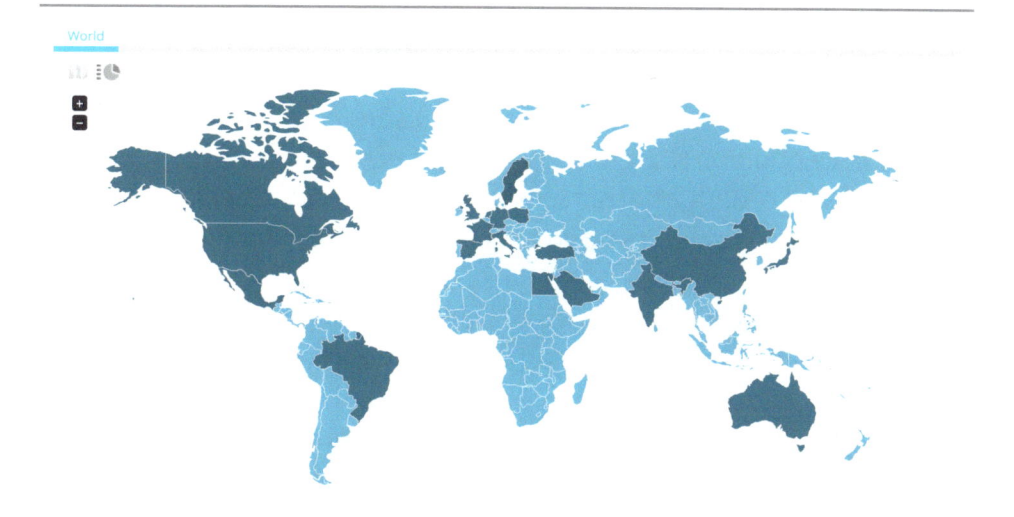

Clicks coming from a country with their own Amazon storefront are often wasted when sent to Amazon.com.

Where to start (and which programs to avoid)

As discussed earlier, the first Amazon affiliate program you should start with should be where the bulk of your audience is coming from. Now, your goal is to sign up for additional international Amazon affiliate programs where you see significant traffic. This will likely be slightly different for every site, however, this is the typical game plan one might use:

Most of our clients start with Amazon.com because they are either US-based, their audience is primarily US-based, and/or they are creating content in English. If you haven't already signed up for the US/Amazon.com program, do so now because it's the largest store.

The next affiliate programs to sign up for are in the main English speaking countries. Creators typically turn next to Canada (amazon.ca), followed closely by the UK (amazon.co.uk) and then Australia (amazon.com.au).

However, with the new "Earn Globally" initiative inside the Amazon.com Associates Central Dashboard it's nearly seamless to enable affiliation from the Canadian, United Kingdom, French, Spanish, German, and Italian affiliate programs. This might be an easier path if Australia isn't a high percentage of your traffic.

If the US / Amazon.com Associates program wasn't your first choice and the UK or multiple European countries are next on your list, one trick in simplifying the signup process is to first sign up with the Amazon UK program so that you can then automatically apply the same information to the four "core" programs in Europe: Germany, Italy, France, and Spain. This makes the sign-up process significantly faster, but not as fast as leveraging the new "Earn Globally" path.

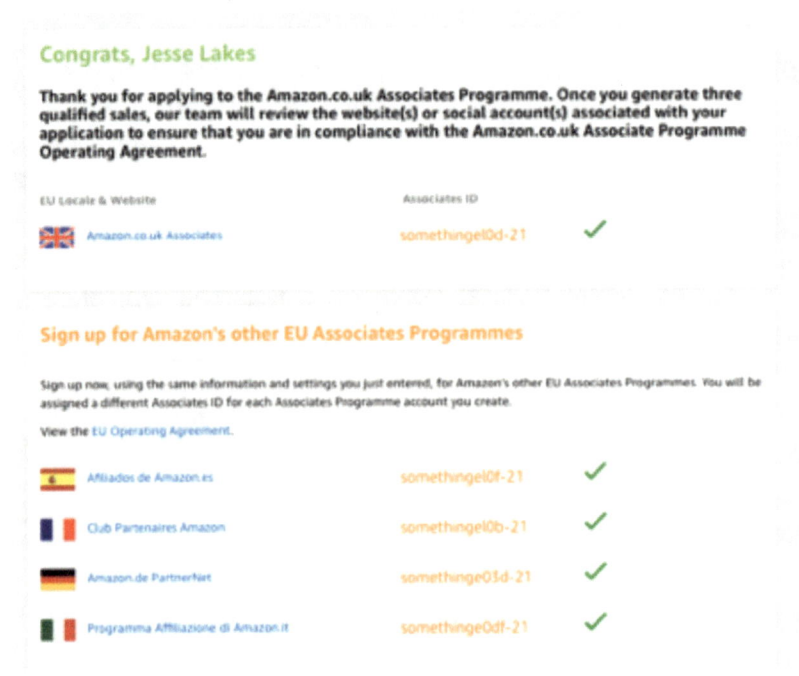

Starting with Amazon UK's affiliate program can save you a few minutes by automatically signing you up for the French, German, Italian, and Spanish programs.

The next affiliate programs typically signed up for include Amazon.co.jp (Japan) and Amazon.com.au (Australia). With the more recent launches of affiliate programs for Amazon.ae (UAE), Amazon.sg (Singapore), and Amazon.nl (Netherlands).

The affiliate program for Amazon.in (India) is a bit tricky because it doesn't currently provide international payments. We recommend to our clients that if they have a sizable audience from India (greater than 5% of your total traffic), to sign up with Cuelinks to access the Amazon.in program. Cuelinks, an Indian-based sub-affiliate network, can then help deal with the taxes and fees for making international payments for your Amazon.in sales.

Read More!
How to setup Cuelinks for Amazon.in Commissions

The Amazon.cn (China) storefront and affiliate program haven't received much attention in the last few years, and we guess that it won't in the future so we don't recommend putting your efforts here as there are other more meaningful revenue driving opportunities with other countries.

The Amazon.com.mx (Mexico) and Amazon.com.br (Brazil) affiliate programs are similar to India in that they don't currently make international payments. So unless you live there, or know someone who does and is okay with you using their local bank account, then we typically recommend avoiding these programs for now. As a foreigner you can earn commissions but won't be able to actually be paid out your commissions without a local bank account number and/or local business tax ID.

If you have a significant audience from Mexico or Brazil (again, more than 5% of your total traffic comes from either of these countries) it may be worth signing up for the affiliate program so you can earn and accumulate commissions. Then once you hit a critical threshold, use that as a reason to travel to the countries and figure out how to get a bank account opened up so you can deposit your earnings. It's likely you'll need to create a local business entity which could require hiring a local lawyer to craft the necessary paperwork and help you out. This can cost in the range of one thousand to three thousand dollars.

The Amazon.com.tr (Turkey) and Amazon.eg (Egypt) affiliate programs are currently set to private and require an invitation to participate. Living in or having a significant presence in these countries is typically a requirement for getting an invitation to join these programs.

While getting signed up for the international affiliate programs can be a bit of work, each program uses the exact same form and shouldn't take more than 10-20 minutes.

Intelligent links: OneLink vs. Geniuslink

Getting signed up for the international affiliate programs is only part of the battle. You are ready to earn commissions from referrals to each of the storefronts, so now you need to drive sales!

One way to do this is by adding individual links for each Amazon storefront, and having the consumer decide which is best for them. We strongly recommend against this method.

> **D. K. Deters** @dk_deters · Jan 6
> THE TEXAN'S FAVOR
> "…Kat and Jake's paths collide for better or for worse."
> ★★★★★
> tinyurl.com/TTF-Amazon-US
> tinyurl.com/TTF-Amazon-AU
> tinyurl.com/TTF-Amazon-CA
> tinyurl.com/TTF-Amazon-UK
> #wrpbks #Romance #Secondchances #westernromance #westerns #readingcommunity #historicalromance

Do you know which link YOU are supposed to click? What happens if you aren't living in the US, UK, Australia, or Canada?

First, this creates friction in the buying process for all of your consumers, and we often see that conversion actually decreases across the board. Second, it's just ugly and a bad use of your limited characters!

Instead, we strongly recommend using a tool specialized in exactly this -- sending every click to the appropriate product in the Amazon storefront that is local for the shopper clicking the link.

There are two major options for this type of tool: Geniuslink and Amazon OneLink, in addition to a number of Amazon affiliate-focused WordPress plugins that provide more simplistic versions of Geniuslink or OneLink.

Amazon OneLink

Amazon introduced a solution to its "geo-fragmentation" challenge in July 2017 via a javascript-based tool. Initially just supporting the translation of amazon.com links to amazon.ca (Canada) and amazon.co.uk (UK), OneLink later expanded to include amazon.de (Germany), amazon.fr (France), amazon.es (Spain), amazon.it (Italy), and amazon.co.jp (Japan).

Going Global With Your Affiliate Links

Now monetize your international traffic from Europe and Japan

OneLink now monetizes traffic from United Kingdom, Canada, Italy, France, Spain, Germany, Japan and neighboring countries

The tool was enhanced again a few years later, and currently supports 13 regions. In the last few months, Amazon has also expanded OneLink from only supporting the translation of Amazon.com links to also expanding to support links from the roughly 13 storefronts that match the 13 affiliate programs the service works with.

OneLink is found in the Amazon Associates Central dashboard under the Tools drop-down.

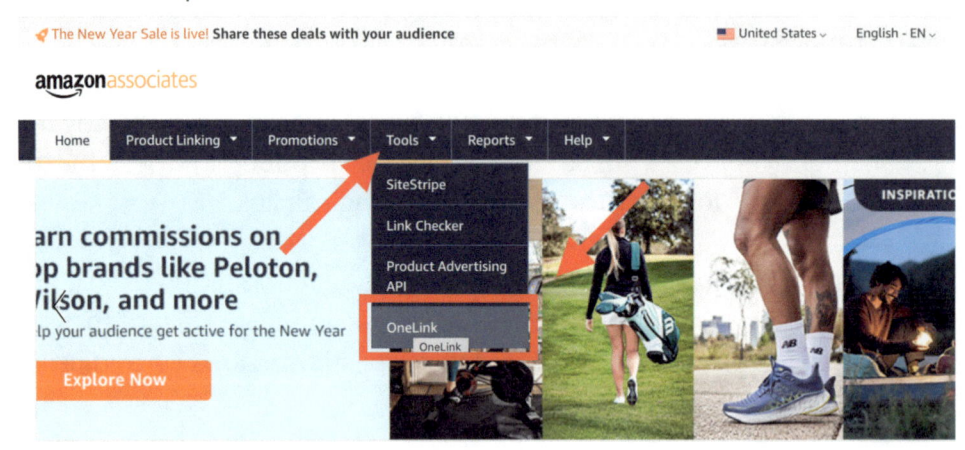

From there you can start the process of mapping your account in the other storefronts / affiliate programs, setting up which tracking IDs are to be used, and what degree of accuracy in matching you'd prefer.

With one of the more recent updates, OneLink moved away from being Javascript based so the tool can now configure any of the Amazon affiliate links you've placed, at any point, that belong to that account.

The tool is built into Amazon so all the configuration can be done inside the Associates Central dashboard.

You can take advantage of the Consolidated Reporting, reporting from other international Associates accounts that use the same email address, and earn globally using your same Amazon.com tracking IDs for other countries, without having to turn on and use OneLink. This fairly recent addition allows for you to mix and match best in class tools.

OneLink tool is offered for free by Amazon, and its product translation is fairly robust, especially in comparison to the other tools that existed in the space at launch.

Unfortunately, the OneLink tool has some significant downfalls including...

Defaulting to Search Links

OneLink just doesn't do a great job finding the same product, in a foreign storefront, that you are linking to. As a result a sizable percentage (57% in our last round of testing) link to search results pages. We believe this happens because Amazon's matching rules don't do well when a product has a different ASIN in a foreign storefront or detailed matching rules to catch many of the nuances surrounding Amazon's product catalog.

Unfortunately, search results pages have a lower conversion rate and Amazon pays a lower commission rate on links that lead to a search results page in the core programs across Europe[30]. This means that using OneLink can lead to a lower international payout rate.

---

[30] https://geni.us/affiliateearnings

Lack of Customization

OneLink is pretty simple, for the most part it's on or it's off. You don't get much control over the functionality or options to improve the subpar matching.

Limited Coverage

Although the coverage of OneLink has radically improved in the last handful of years, it's still quite limited in comparison to the full breadth of Amazon's greater affiliate program.

Geniuslink

As one of the first tools to support linking to online stores with international storefronts and affiliate programs, we started supporting the Amazon affiliate program with auto-affiliation and link localization in mid-2013. In the last ten years, we've continued to improve on the service and link translation and are now the premium provider and largest independent Amazon affiliate link management platform. The Geniuslink service is used by many thousands of Amazon affiliate publishers, creators, and influencers of all sizes.

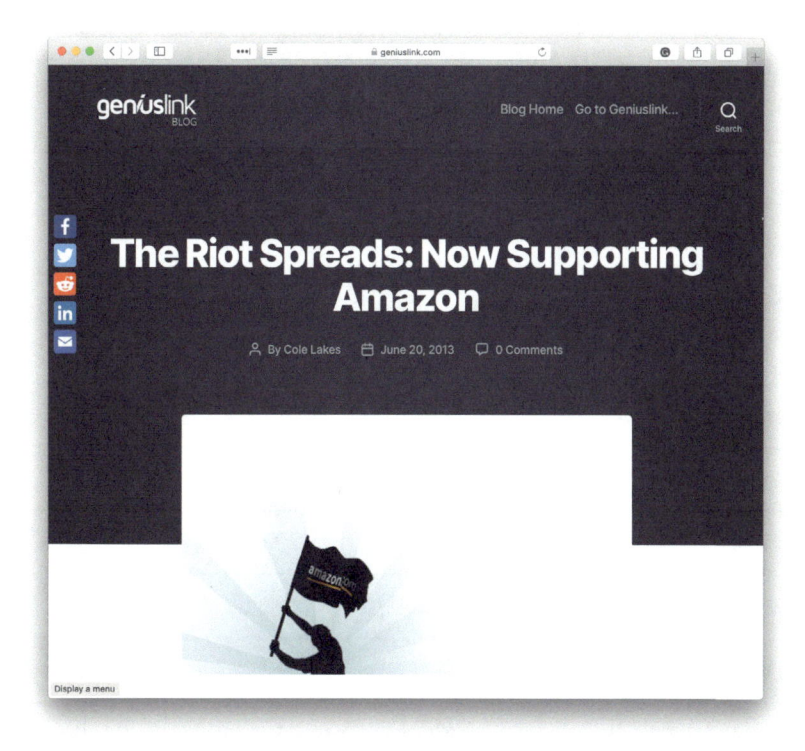

Ten years ago we (Geniuslink) started to support Amazon's affiliate programs.

To be transparent, Geniuslink is available for a nominal monthly fee, based on usage, whereas OneLink is offered for free by Amazon. However, in comparison to OneLink, Geniuslink really shines (but I'm biased).

Product Matching Accuracy

The goal of using a link localization tool is to get your international visitors to the right product in their local Amazon storefront so they can easily buy. Doing this well can significantly increase your total commissions without any increase in your traffic, but using a sub-par service with low accuracy can drastically lower your commissions.

We regularly test the Geniuslink match accuracy to that of OneLink and over the years the results have consistently shown our service is dominant. More details on how we run our tests, the methodology behind the scoring, and our safeguards to reduce any implied bias can be found in our blog: Link Localization Testing: Amazon OneLink vs. Genius Link[31].

Period	Products tested	Geniuslink Score	OneLink Score	Difference
Summer 2021	3,119	1,039 (33.3%)	477.5 (15.3%)	118%
Spring 2020	1,115	622 (55.8%)	422.5 (37.9%)	47%
Spring 2018	840	389 (46.3%)	292 (34.8%)	33%
Winter 2018	840	304 (36.2%)	198 (23.6%)	54%
Fall 2017	840	409 (48.7%)	327 (38.9%)	25%
Summer 2017	160	90 (56.3%)	41 (25.6%)	120%

Link Customization

With OneLink, you are stuck with their international destinations, even if they are wrong. With Geniuslink, you have complete control over how a link functions, allowing you to fully customize the performance when the programmatic localization isn't perfect.

Coverage

There are a couple places where OneLink and Geniuslink greatly differ.

---

[31] https://geni.us/onelinkvsgeniuslink

The **number of storefronts supported** is the first. Geniuslink can translate any Amazon link, regardless of which storefront it originated at, to any Amazon store (with the sole exception being Turkey). This means we can start with 21 link formats (one for each store as well as for amzn.to) and redirect to 21 different Amazon stores while OneLink is limited to 13 link formats/storefronts.

Further, Geniuslink provides link localization for Amazon links that are not affiliated! This is super helpful for creators that wish to put Amazon links behind QR codes in printed material, in PDFs, backmatter of books, or in email, all areas where Amazon has forbidden their affiliate links to be used.

The second, is the **type of links that are supported**. In short, OneLink doesn't support the localization of search links or landing pages. This means that OneLink does not help you earn bounties from services, seasonal landing pages (e.g. Black Friday and Prime Day), or other offers on Amazon while Geniuslink has you covered.[32]

Features

The next major distinction between Geniuslink and OneLink involves the features that a premium link management tool offers.

Knowing how your links are performing is pretty important which makes **reporting** a key feature. Amazon Associates Central is currently the only dashboard where you can get sales and commission reporting from your affiliate efforts. Outside of that,

---

[32] https://geni.us/amazonhva

the reporting available is pretty limited. The biggest bit of missing data is knowing where your clicks are coming from and where they are going. Geniuslink's reporting excels at this.

As will be discussed further in the coming chapter, **broken links** are a major pain for Amazon's affiliate program. Amazon's product catalog is huge and dynamic. Some links simply break (go to a 404), or the product they are linking to goes out of stock, with no plans to be restocked. Both of these experiences lead to lower conversion rates as they result in a dead-end buying experience.

Next steps

Regardless of the link management tool you choose, after signing up for the international Amazon affiliate programs that correspond with your top countries, decide on the intelligent link management service that works best for you. It's important to implement the service then do the following two things to ensure everything is working correctly:

- **Test your links** - which can be as simple as clicking the link and seeing where you land and the "tag=xxxx-2x" appears.

- **Watch your reports** - log into those international Associates Central dashboards to ensure your international commissions are starting to come through.

After you've let one of the tools help you monetize your international traffic for a few months, it's vital to review your analytics and see if you should be increasing support for additional international Amazon affiliate programs due to growth in your site or channel, or a change in your audience composition.

Advanced Amazon Affiliate Tips

Get a glimpse at advanced optimization tools and techniques to maximize commissions.

See how diversifying your revenue can help boost your Amazon conversions.

Learn about additional ways to recommend products and earn.

Now that you've spent some time learning a handful of best practices, and getting set up to earn commissions internationally to provide a better user experience for your foreign fans, it's time to level up your Amazon affiliate marketing game.

The following seven advanced tactics are focused towards those who have already put in some time growing their content, have seen some traction from their efforts, are focused on building a community, and generate at least a few hundred dollars a month in commissions.

If you haven't quite hit these milestones, you are still welcome to dive in and continue learning while you focus on building up your content and community.

Broken Amazon affiliate links

Just like the rest of the internet, links to products on Amazon can "rot," and this can be a major problem for publishers and content creators who have been building Amazon affiliate links over the course of years. A link that goes to Amazon's 404 (Dogs of Amazon) page instead of the product you are recommending isn't going to convert and essentially becomes a wasted click.

Additionally, a link that goes to the correct product but is currently out of stock or no longer being sold is also a wasted effort and will convert at a significantly lower rate, if at all.

Advanced Amazon Affiliate Tips

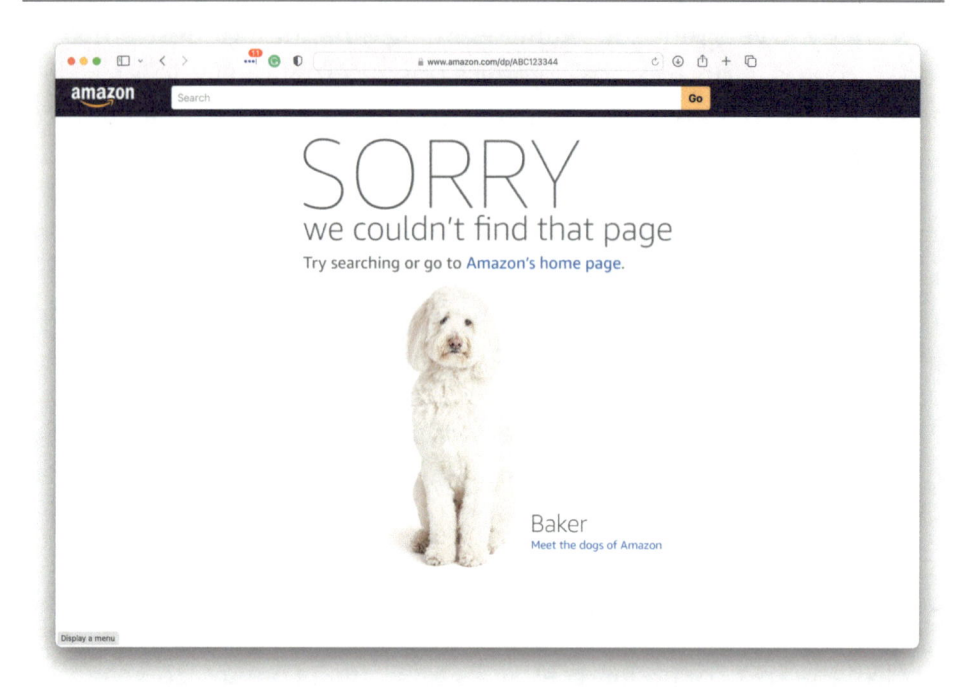

The dogs of Amazon sure are cute but they are horrible for your conversion rate!

We call this "Link Health," and it's often the last thing on someone's mind as they are initially building their content and adding in their affiliate links. While the odds are that the links you just added will "break," or the product goes out of stock, are relatively low, the older your site or channel is, or the more affiliate links you have posted, the higher the odds are.

Finding and fixing these links to ensure proper link health becomes another task to add to your growing list as you continue to up your affiliate marketing game. While it could be as easy as just clicking on all of your links and seeing which ones break, that can be incredibly time-consuming and inefficient.

With the Geniuslink platform, we've built in a link health report (currently in beta) and provide an easy way to update affiliate links that are no longer working, recognized by Amazon's Product Advertising API, or are for products that have gone out of stock.

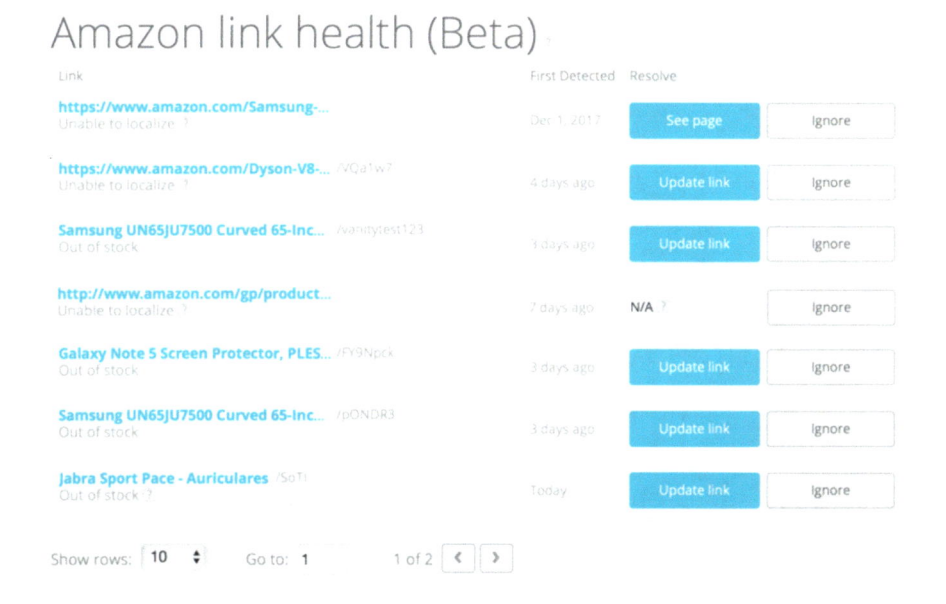

The Amazon link health report in the Geniuslink dashboard shows which links are no longer generating revenue for you (aka "broken").

The Amazon Associates dashboard seems to be slowly introducing a similar feature at the time of this writing, though it is also in beta and it's not consistently available across all accounts. We have also heard reports that it's not very thorough in its reporting. So far this tool in Associates Central doesn't appear to provide any easy process for finding or fixing the link.

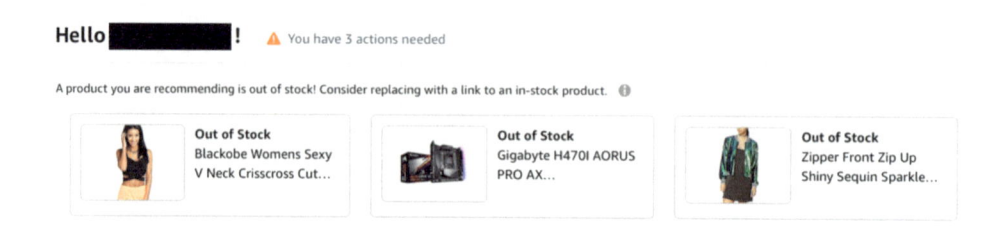

A recently seen "Broken Links" report, found inside the Amazon Associates Central dashboard.

Our favorite third party tool that provides link health reporting, without violating the Associates Operating Agreement[33], is AMZ Watcher (amzwatcher.com).

Using multiple Amazon affiliate tracking IDs

When you first start with the Amazon affiliate program, you are issued an initial affiliate store ID. What many people don't know is you can actually build up to 100 unique tracking IDs in your account, then within your reports, you can filter each by your tracking IDs. These two pieces allow you significantly more granularity in measuring your affiliate efforts to determine what is and isn't working.

As a quick aside, the difference between a "store ID" and a "tracking ID" is that the store ID is the default tracking ID that is issued for your account. Any subsequent tracking IDs created for your account are referred to as a tracking ID. Referring to them all as tracking IDs is common however so feel free to ignore this tidbit.

---

[33] Section 6 of the Operating Agreement says "(s) You will not artificially generate clicks or impressions on your Site or create Sessions on an Amazon Site, whether by way of a robot or software program or otherwise."

Advanced Amazon Affiliate Tips

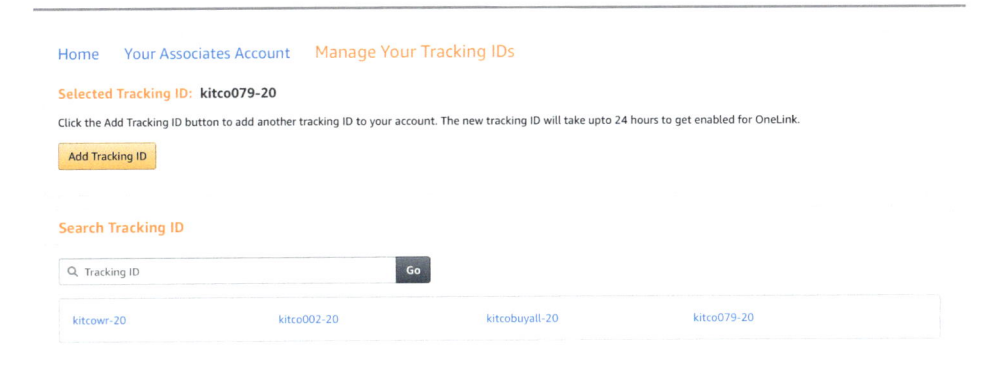

Amazon Associates Central allows you to create up to 100 tracking IDs

The easiest use case for this is to create a new tracking ID for each web property or social media channel that you create, so you can measure how each performs in comparison. This might mean that for your YouTube channel you use "youtubeabc-20" and for your blog about cats, you create the tracking id "catsite123-20" and finally, your viral dog video website could use "dogvidsxyz-20".

Now that your three channels have three different tracking IDs, you can jump into the Amazon Associates Central dashboard and look at your clicks, sales, and commissions on a per tracking ID, aka per digital property, basis to start to determine what is and isn't working.

You may find your YouTube channel gets the least clicks but converts at the highest rate, or that your earnings per click for the viral dog video is half of what the cat blog generates, or that your cat blog has a lot of sales for cat backpacks when that isn't something you've ever written about.

In each of these, there are actionable insights that can help you focus your time and efforts to refine your strategy; where having all of your links, across all of your channels, would have only given you a blended idea of your clicks, sales, commissions, EPC and conversion rates.

Note that you might find that a well-organized spreadsheet is really helpful here.

Within Geniuslink, we use a system called Groups and Overrides[34] to allow clients to easily ensure the correct tracking information is used with each link.

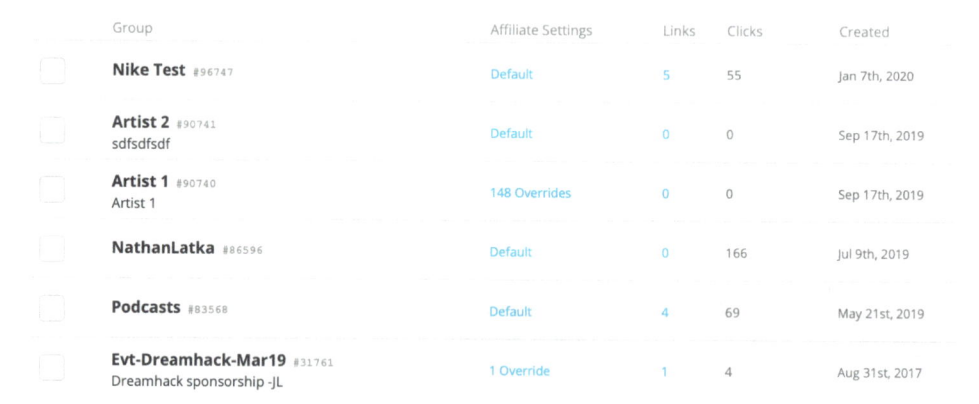

Group	Affiliate Settings	Links	Clicks	Created
Nike Test #96747	Default	5	55	Jan 7th, 2020
Artist 2 #90741 sdfsdfsdf	Default	0	0	Sep 17th, 2019
Artist 1 #90740 Artist 1	148 Overrides	0	0	Sep 17th, 2019
NathanLatka #86596	Default	0	166	Jul 9th, 2019
Podcasts #83568	Default	4	69	May 21st, 2019
Evt-Dreamhack-Mar19 #31761 Dreamhack sponsorship -JL	1 Override	1	4	Aug 31st, 2017

Inside the Geniuslink dashboard, you can create groups of links then assign specific affiliate tracking IDs to these links (which is called creating affiliate overrides).

Mobile Deep Links

A "deep link" simply refers to linking to a specific product or page inside a store (versus just linking to the main "home" page of the store).

However, a "**mobile deep link**" is a link that when clicked on from inside an app (like the Facebook or YouTube app), has some extra smarts that will first try and redirect directly into the Amazon app instead of letting the mobile device decide how the link should resolve. This is often the ideal user experience as it leads shoppers to the

---

[34] https://geni.us/groupsoverrides

environment where they are most comfortable buying from (typically because they are already logged in/have their credit card details saved.

It takes some careful observation but most links when clicked from inside an app often end up in that app's built-in browser or the default mobile browser on the device (Safari or Chrome).

The problem with either the app's browser or the built-in browser loading the Amazon page is that the odds are fairly high that the shopper isn't "logged in" on the Amazon site. Thus there is an extra, often major, hurdle in actually buying the product you recommended -- logging in.

However, if someone has the Amazon app installed on their phone (and nearly 100 million people in the US[35] roughly ⅓ of the total population do) then they are likely already logged in which means it's way easier for them to buy.

Our testing of the mobile deep linking technology built into Geniuslink shows that from YouTube these "smart" links increased conversion rates anywhere from 5X to 8X! Note, however, this increase only applies to mobile based clicks. Mobile Deep Links don't add any value for clicks coming outside of mobile devices.

However, this isn't always the case! Some product types, digital media in particular, aren't actually available to buy from within the Amazon app. For example, you can't buy a Kindle ebook or an audiobook from within the Amazon app. For these products a mobile deep link is actually a worse user experience.

---

[35] https://geni.us/amazonappusage

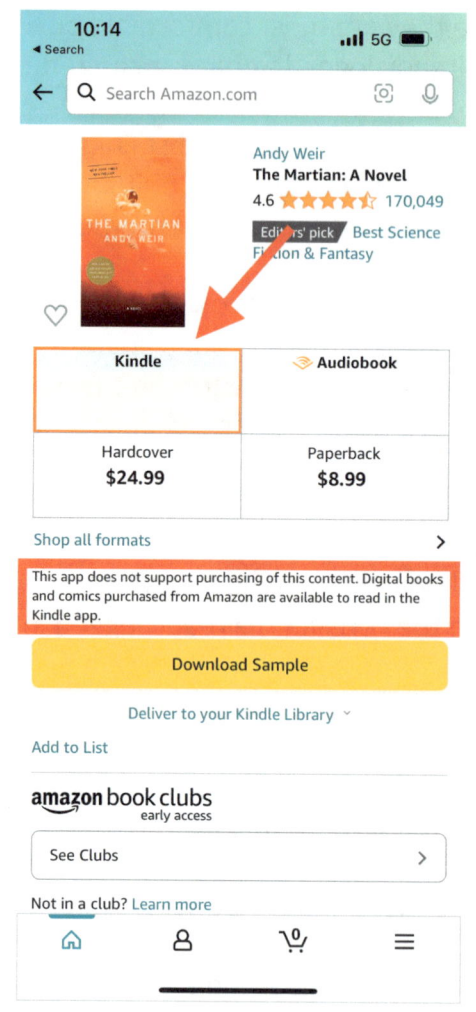

The Amazon app doesn't support sales of digital products. On a mobile device loading the Amazon store in the web browser seems to be the only way to buy these types of products.

This was a lesson the Geniuslink team quickly learned and our links won't mobile deep link for the product types that are negatively affected by the direct to app user experience.

A couple other linking tools that support mobile deep links for Amazon include **URLgenius** and **Button**.

A/B testing your affiliate links

While you should always test your affiliate links to ensure they are acting like they should and include your affiliate tracking information, you can level up by starting to perform A/B testing with your affiliate links to incrementally increase your conversion rates and boost your affiliate revenue.

From one perspective, A/B testing your Amazon affiliate links means experimenting with the visual components of your link. This can include adjusting your call to action (be sure not to inadvertently create an "incentivized" situation!), the treatment of the link (font type, size, color, etc.), and the location of the affiliate links.

There are a number of tools that can help you run multiple versions of a single webpage at the same time, including a free tool provided by Google called "Optimize"[36].

The other option in A/B testing for Amazon affiliate links deals with changing the destination of your link. Options here include testing if a link directly to the product details page converts better than a search results page for the product. It is always good to test the products you are recommending with your audience, but we've found the product details page is typically your best bet and results in the highest commissions.

For some products, like cameras, you can test if the link to the specific product converts better or if you have more luck with a camera that includes a bundle (like a case, lens, filters, memory cards, etc.). Finally, you can also test which retailer converts best -- it may not be Amazon after all!

---

[36] https://geni.us/abtesttool

The Geniuslink platform includes the ability to do A/B testing with link destinations, a feature we regularly use in our own research.

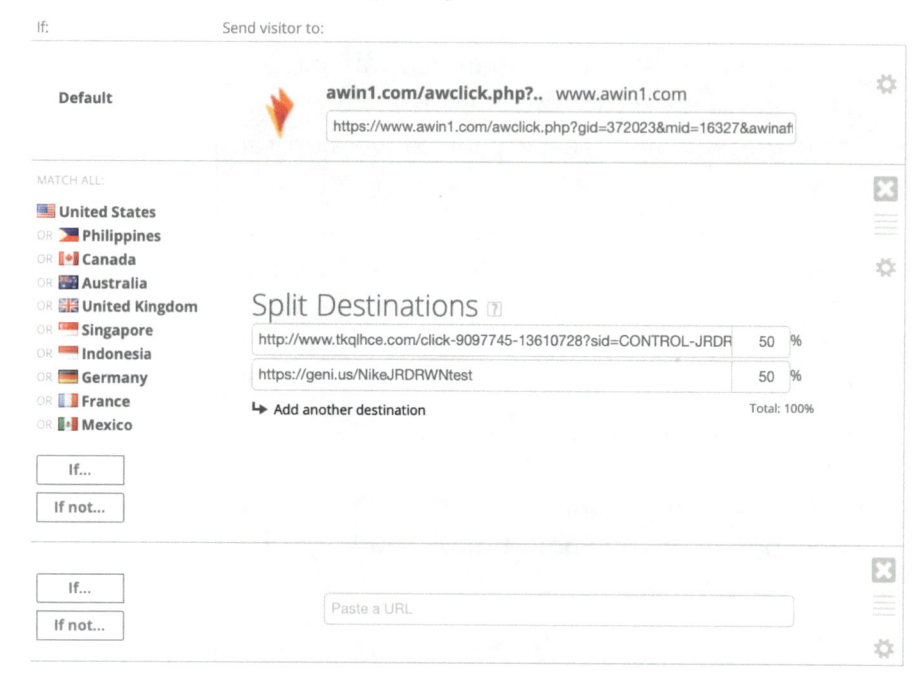

Using a combination of Advanced Targets and A/B links you can configure a test with a very specific use case. Above a select set of countries will have their links split 50/50 between two different destinations while all clicks that don't originate from one of the defined countries go to a separate destination in order to not skew the results of the test.

When you are doing these A/B tests, it's important to be as scientific as possible. This includes paying attention to the details, taking notes on the process, testing only one change at a time, running the experiment with a test and control version at the same time, and having

Read More!
How to Run Experiments to Boost Your Commissions

enough traffic/clicks/sales that your results are as close to statistically significant as possible.

Using multiple affiliate programs

While we firmly believe that Amazon's affiliate program is the best place to start, and one of the best affiliate programs in the world, it certainly isn't the only affiliate program. In fact, we strongly encourage you to start using multiple affiliate programs after you've gotten the hang of how the process works. We call this the **Multi-Retailer**

Approach. Doing so often yields some unexpected, but positive, benefits to your affiliate game.

Amazon doesn't sell everything

The first reason to use multiple affiliate programs is that while Amazon sells *almost* everything, they don't sell everything! Amazon is primarily limited to consumer packaged products as well as physical and digital products. You'll often find some of your favorite tools and services also have a great affiliate or referral program that can be helpful to recommend to your audience.

On the flip side, with a few exceptions for their proprietary products and brands, *almost* everything that is sold on Amazon is also available from other retailers.

Better conversion, commission rates, cookie windows, or terms

In general, Amazon's affiliate program has solid conversion rates due to the massive number of products they sell and the easy ability to earn halo commissions. But their cookie window is relatively short at just 24 hours, and their terms are quite restrictive in comparison with peers.

While the Amazon affiliate program offers decent commission rates, we recently mapped the past decade of Amazon.com affiliate commission rates and have seen a steady decline. You may find that specialty retailers for the products you promote have better commission rates, which can equate to a higher EPC (earnings per click) or total commissions at the end of the day.

You will also find that the 24-hour cookie window is the very low side of the industry, with many other retailers offering 3- to 7-day windows.

Alternatively, other affiliate programs may provide better terms and benefits. Many affiliate programs are okay with you using their affiliate links inside of emails or within an ad. Programs like B&H Photo Video offer a loaner program to their affiliates where they can check out, use, and review many of the high-end products available for sale in B&H's store all for free.

Diversifying your revenue

Only using Amazon's affiliate program is akin to putting all of your eggs in one basket. It makes things simple and allows you to move fast, especially in the early days, but it can be incredibly risky in the long run. We have seen too many people have their revenue completely decimated due to some unforeseen circumstance such as Amazon lowering their commission rates or an inadvertent violation of Amazon's operating agreement with very limited options going forward.

Boost your Amazon commissions

Unexpectedly, we've also found that by including Amazon along with a handful of other retailers selling the same product you can actually boost your conversions and commissions with Amazon.

From what we've gathered, by providing affiliate links to other retailers selling the same product, an interested consumer is (indirectly) encouraged to do all their research upfront. This keeps them from having to leave your site to check out information elsewhere (and cannibalize your traffic).

Clicking the links to see the product's price and availability at multiple stores helps them feel confident moving forward with the purchase. Subtly encouraging them to do their research, by putting the links to do so right in front of them, helps them build momentum (we've heard this tactic being referred to as "micro-conversions"). As a result, the conversion rates and total revenue are often higher when including multiple buying options instead of just using Amazon.

We aren't alone in this discovery. You'll find that some of the biggest players in the affiliate space use the same tactic when they do product reviews.

Additional benefits to a Multi-Retailer approach
Outside of the items listed above there is another handful of reasons to adopt a Multi-Retailer approach that include:

- **Mitigating Supply Chain and Out of Stock issues** - It's not news that our favorite stores just don't have all of our favorite things in stock all the time like they used to. Blame it on COVID, or big ships getting stuck in small channels, a shortage of workers, or about 100 other things; but sending someone to a store that doesn't have the product you are recommending in stock is a dead-end buying experience and your conversion rate is likely to go to zero.

- **Comparison / Bargain Shopping** – While there is some shopper loyalty still out there (Amazon Prime was a brilliant idea), finding the cheapest price is often still the M.O. of many shoppers, especially for higher-priced items. Turns out 78% of shoppers say they like to do comparison shopping[37] and 81% of consumers conduct online research before making a purchase online[38].

---

[37] https://geni.us/bargainshopping
[38] https://geni.us/researchfirst

- **Capturing the other 60% of the market** – Amazon is huge, especially here in the US. Emarketer has them pegged at 40.4% of the US e-commerce market share, with Walmart next at 7%[39]. BUT while 40% is huge that still means that 60% of e-commerce happens outside of Amazon. That's the equivalent of 3 out of every 5 dollars spent online happening elsewhere. Seems like a pretty huge piece of the pie to be missing out on, right? A Multi-Retailer approach to affiliate marketing helps you capture more of the market!

- **Industry Best Practice** – What do CNET, Wirecutter, Digital Trends, and Tom's Guide all have in common besides being some of the biggest names in product reviews and making a ton of money from affiliate marketing? They have all adopted a Multi-Retailer approach to affiliate marketing and rarely exclude other retailers besides Amazon when making a product recommendation.

- **Google is recommending the practice** - In an update in Dec of 2021, Google announced that this strategy is one of the factors to determine how helpful your site/videos are to a person searching for information, and thus where you will sit on a search results page.[40]

---

[39] https://geni.us/marketshare
[40] https://geni.us/googlemultiretailer

Choice Pages

We've been working hard on a tool to help you diversify your affiliate revenue, boost your Amazon commissions, provide a simple solution to some of Amazon's compliance challenges, and ensure full compliance with the FTC and Amazon disclosure requests. We call these **Choice Pages**.

They are easy to build, simple, and elegant landing pages that allow you to recommend a single product across multiple retailers via a short link that can be used anywhere and should be used everywhere.

Advanced Amazon Affiliate Tips

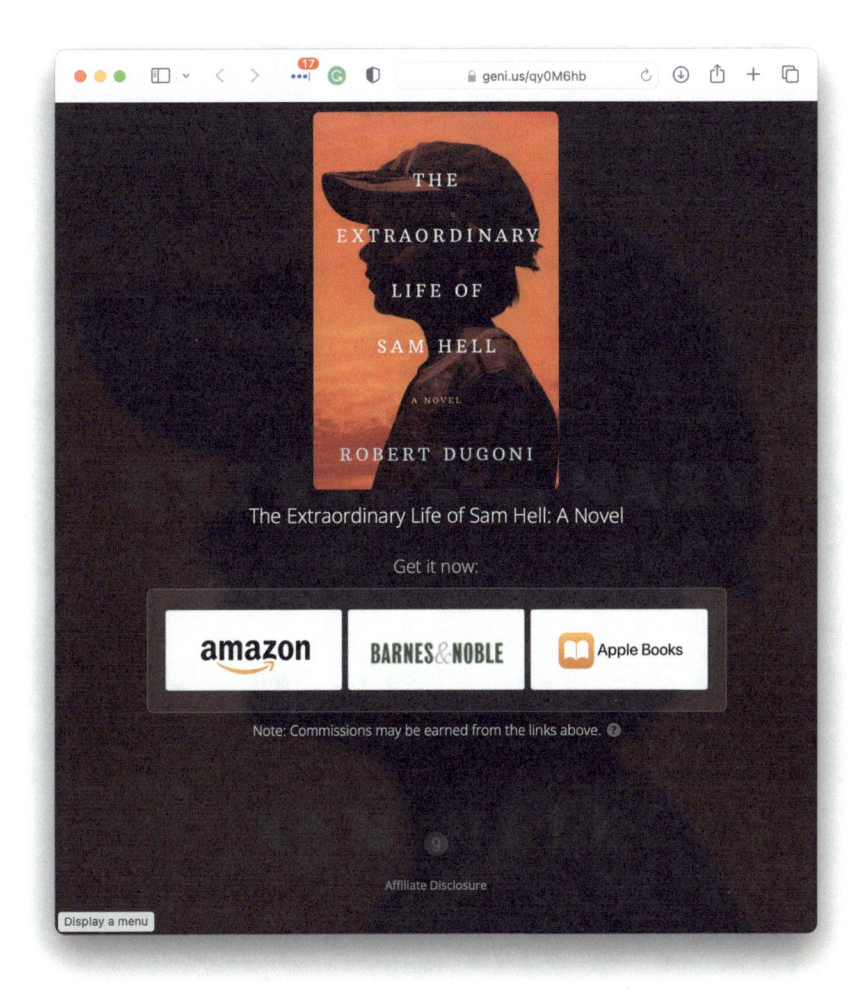

A Choice Page promotes a product via multiple retailers in a clean landing page.

Product curation via Kit

At the end of the day, your job as an Amazon affiliate marketer is to curate the best products in a certain niche and share those with your audience.

Advanced Amazon Affiliate Tips

You can do that across your website, blog, and social media. You can also do that with Kit.co, a newer social media platform specifically designed for curating and sharing products with an emphasis on affiliate marketing.

Expanding your product curation efforts past your current digital properties, and onto Kit, allows you a concise way to bundle products for your audience and allows you to be discovered by consumers looking for exactly the types of products in your area of expertise.

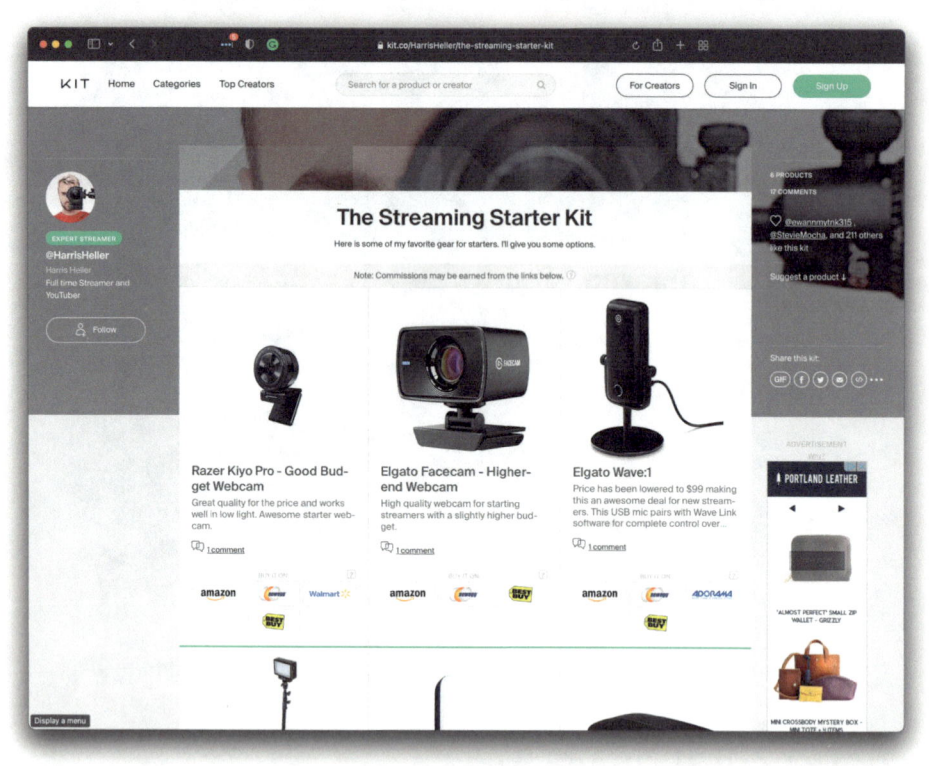

A kit shows off a creator's favorite products to solve a problem with clean art and multiple buy buttons to help boost conversion rates and commissions.

Kit also adopts the "multi-retailer" approach similar to Choice Pages to help you maximize your affiliate commissions. Approximately two dozen other well-known and reputable affiliate programs are supported by Kit to ensure your recommendations are being fully monetized.

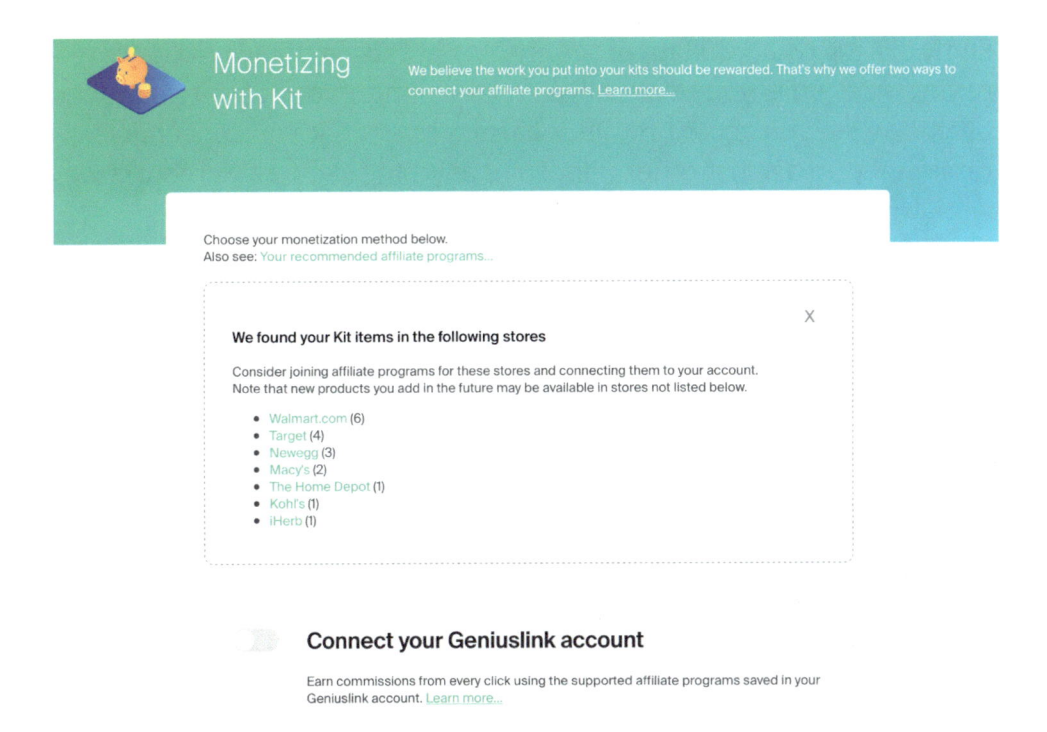

Your Kit account can support adding in your affiliate tracking info or connecting your Geniuslink account for more flexibility.

The Kit dashboard also allows you to add in your affiliate tracking information for the majority of Amazon's affiliate programs worldwide so that your recommendation's links to Amazon will include your affiliate tracking IDs. This is a great opportunity to create new tracking IDs (as discussed in the second section of this chapter) so you can compare the performance of Kit to your existing properties and marketing campaigns.

Are you under or overperforming?

You probably track your affiliate commissions like a hawk. You likely know exactly what affiliate programs you are using and what they are paying. And while you might have an idea of how your earnings change over time, do you know how your earnings per click and conversion rates stack up against others? If you're anything like many creators we work with, the answer is probably not.

While everyone will see different EPCs and conversion rates from their links and campaigns, we wanted to share what we see for Amazon's affiliate program so you can use it as a single additional data point for a rough baseline in comparison.

We've pulled the Q1 2022 (January through March) clicks, sales, and commissions data from the 17 Amazon Associates programs that we work with for Kit.co and calculated the EPC and conversion rates.

Before digging into these numbers it's important to note that your numbers may be very different and **you should NOT judge your efforts as a success or failure solely based on these numbers.** Use this data simply as an additional data point.

Further, **context always matters**, and you know your audience best! If your niche and audience are similar to our creators, you should be able to use this as a guide as you experiment with the best programs to maximize your earnings.

And of course, **take everything with a grain of salt**!

Program	EPC	Conversion Rate
Amazon.com	$0.124	9.13%
Amazon.ca	$0.150	7.01%
Amazon.com.mx	$0.110	4.34%
Amazon.com.br	$0.011	0.83%
Amazon.co.uk	$0.037	3.97%
Amazon.de	$0.054	5.99%
Amazon.fr	$0.064	4.95%
Amazon.es	$0.031	3.52%
Amazon.it	$0.026	2.53%
Amazon.nl	$0.093	2.73%
Amazon.se	$0.080	3.29%
Amazon.pl	$0.022	0.97%
Amazon.sa	$0.040	2.16%
Amazon.ae	$0.070	4.30%
Amazon.co.jp	$0.044	5.38%
Amazon.sg	$0.046	1.84%
Amazon.com.au	$0.095	4.15%

A quick reminder that EPC is calculated as your earnings (your commissions, not the total value of the sales) divided by your clicks. Further, different services count clicks in different ways so make sure you are consistent in where you grab your denominator!

The conversion rate is calculated as the number of products sold divided by your clicks. This too can be a little confusing when comparing the data above to other programs as most affiliate programs use the total number of orders, not products sold.

So how does Amazon's affiliate program stack up against other affiliate programs?

Funny you ask, we've explored this too, and while it's not a true "apples to apples" comparison with Kit we've found Amazon.com's conversion rate to be the best of all + 20 other affiliate programs that we compared it to. Amazon comes in at about 3X higher than the next best program, Apple Services, and 5X higher than the average conversion rate. A combination of all of the Amazon affiliate programs still had an incredible conversion rate with twice that of Apple Services and 3X the average conversion rates.

EPCs were a bit lower in comparison with Amazon.com coming in third in our comparison and a blend of all of the Amazon affiliate programs together was a bit further down but still in the top 10.

When comparing Amazon to other affiliate programs the calculations were slightly different as we had to normalize clicks across the various affiliate programs so we divided commissions and sales by our (Geniuslink) click counts as it seems every reporting platform has a different way to differentiate an organic click versus a junk click.

It's also important to note that Kit incorporates Geniuslink for premium geo-targeting and link localization for Amazon links and adopts a Multi-Retailer approach which has also proven to boost conversion rates (and commissions!).

If you are interested in learning more about our explorations on comparing EPC and conversion rates check out our blog: Under or Over Performing (https://geni.us/programcomparison).

Exit your Amazon affiliate business

While setting up your Amazon affiliate website to be a long-term, sustainable, and passive income business is often the goal, you may find the ultimate -- and best -- payout is when you sell it!

There is absolutely nothing wrong with building up an Amazon affiliate-focused website, getting it to a certain size in terms of traffic or affiliate commissions, and then letting it coast while you focus on other things.

But just like we discussed above with link health and declining commission rates, you may find that your "passive" business is not really passive. Add in other factors like Google's regularly changing search engine algorithm updates, Facebook's tweaks and friendliness towards external links, or YouTube's head-scratching moves, and you may find that momentum often dies quicker than you'd like.

Often the best move for your Amazon affiliate business, after you've put the time and effort into it that you feel is right, is to sell it.

Website buyers come in all shapes and sizes including major Private Equity firms and other major web publishers to brand new solo entrepreneurs excited to leave their day job for something where they are in control of their destiny.

Buyers are also looking for all sizes of websites. As long as your website can consistently bring in tens to hundreds of dollars of affiliate commissions each month you've got the potential to sell it.

Amazon is perfectly fine with you selling your digital properties, but they do have some concerns around allowing secondary-user access to

Advanced Amazon Affiliate Tips

your Associates account, and you are not permitted to sell your Associates account. Rather the buyer of your site should create their own Amazon affiliate account and then replace the tracking ID on the affiliate links in your site with theirs (surprise, surprise, Geniuslink makes this super easy!).

Amazon affiliate websites are often priced at a "multiple" of what your monthly affiliate revenue is. The greater market is responsible for setting what this multiple is but a rule of thumb is to use around 20x (+/- 5) although this varies depending on multiple factors. A good broker can help you navigate these waters.

There are multiple platforms you can use to get the word out that you are looking to sell your website. Typically the platform you would find most beneficial to use is correlated to what your monthly revenue is. Here are a few of our favorites:

Lower monthly revenue (tens, hundreds, to low thousands of dollars per month) are likely best suited for listing on a service like **Flippa** (flippa.com).

Middle tier monthly revenue (thousands to mid/high tens of thousands) is likely more suited for a service like **Motion Invest** (motioninvest.com) or **Empire Flippers** (empireflippers.com).

High tier monthly revenue (high five, six, seven, and eight figure monthly revenues) would likely best be served by brokerages like **Quiet Light** (QuietLight.com) and **FE International** (feinternational.com).

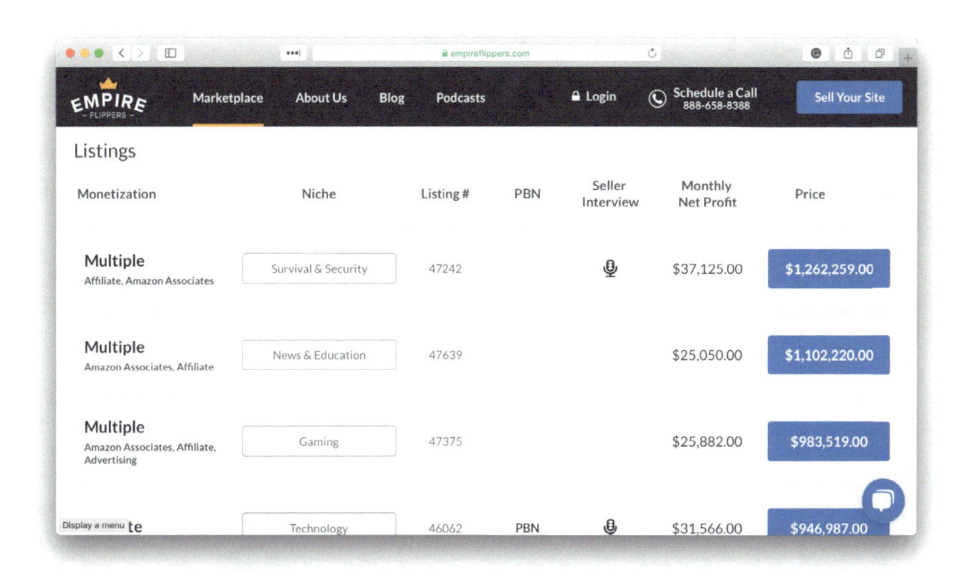

Listings from the Empire Flippers site shows the Monthly Net Profit and the list price for the property.

As with any business an entrepreneur builds, it becomes their baby. And while hard to say goodbye, the ultimate milestone for the entrepreneurial journey is exiting the business.

Wrapping Up

Thank you!

Any questions, comments, or feedback?

How to get an extended free trial with Geniuslink.

Thank you!

First, a huge thank you, to you, the reader! I hope that you picked up some good nuggets along the way and are ready to take your Amazon affiliate game to the next level.

It's also important to thank the tens of thousands of creators, across our three platforms, that trust in us to help ensure continued success with their affiliate links. But even more importantly, a huge thanks to all of them for giving us a chance to learn the nuances of their business and the Amazon Associates Program from their perspective. Our clients are the most wonderful teachers and we really appreciate the opportunity they provide us.

Finally, a massive thank you to Geniuslink team members both past and present. You are all amazing at what you do, and we have been able to move mountains together as a team - all while navigating uncertain territory -- and every moment has been worth it! I appreciate every one of you!

Questions? Ping me...

If you haven't noticed, I love this stuff! If you have any questions, comments, concerns, or feedback about anything in this book or the Amazon Associates Program in general please don't hesitate to reach out. You can hit me up at jl@geni.us (yes, that's my personal email and I'll personally respond) or you can reach the Geniuslink team at hi@geni.us. We look forward to hearing from you!

What did we miss?

We are aiming to make regular updates to this book and encourage you to help us shape the future of it. What topics did we miss? Where would you have liked us to go a bit deeper? Help us improve future versions of this book and we'll happily acknowledge you for your contributions, and hook you up with a Geniuslink account credit!

Our gift to you

Did we happen to pique your curiosity about Geniuslink? Want to check it out? We'd be delighted to have you!

For an extended free trial, ping us at help@geni.us with your (new) Geniuslink user name or the email address you used to set up the account along with the page number in the book you saw in this note and we'll double your free trial (from 14 days to a month). If you send us a picture of you holding the book, we'll extend your free trial from 14 days to two months!

If you already have a Geniuslink account we can still hook you up! Please send us a copy of your receipt from buying this book and we'll add the price of the book as credit in your account. We'll double that if you also send along a picture of you with the book.

Best of luck!

The Amazon Associates Program can be a roller coaster but hopefully, you've picked up on some of the mistakes I've made and learned the lessons that took me decades, so you can reach the top much quicker. Regardless of where you are on the ride, hang on, have fun and just remember the best way to learn is to dive right in and get your hands dirty.

From my team to yours, we wish you the best of luck in your adventures!

Appendix A -
Amazon Storefronts and Affiliate Programs Worldwide

Appendix A - Amazon Storefronts and Affiliate Programs Worldwide

As of January 2023 Amazon's "ecosystem" consisted of the following storefronts and affiliate programs.

Region	Country	Store	Affiliate / Associates Program Signup	Public / Private
N. America	US	Amazon.com	https://affiliate-program.amazon.com/	Public
N. America	Canada	Amazon.ca	https://associates.amazon.ca/	Public
N. America	Mexico	Amazon.com.mx	https://afiliados.amazon.com.mx/	Public
S. America	Brazil	Amazon.com.br	https://associados.amazon.com.br/	Public
Europe	United Kingdom	Amazon.co.uk	https://affiliate-program.amazon.co.uk/	Public
Europe	Germany	Amazon.de	https://partnernet.amazon.de/	Public
Europe	France	Amazon.fr	https://partenaires.amazon.fr/	Public
Europe	Spain	Amazon.es	https://afiliados.amazon.es/	Public
Europe	Italy	Amazon.it	https://programma-affiliazione.amazon.it/	Public
Europe	Netherlands	Amazon.nl	https://partnernet.amazon.nl/	Public
Europe	Sweden	Amazon.se	https://affiliate-program.amazon.se/	Public
Europe	Poland	Amazon.pl	https://affiliate-program.amazon.pl/	Public
Europe	Turkey	Amazon.com.tr	https://gelirortakligi.amazon.com.tr/	**Private**
Europe	Belgium	Amazon.com.be	https://affiliate-program.amazon.com.be	Public
Middle East	Saudia Arabia	Amazon.sa	https://affiliate-program.amazon.sa/	Public
Middle East	United Arab Emirates	Amazon.ae	https://affiliate-program.amazon.ae/	**Public**
Middle East	Egypt	Amazon.eg	https://affiliate-program.amazon.eg/	Private
Asia	India	Amazon.in	https://affiliate-program.amazon.in/	Public
Asia	China	Amazon.cn	https://associates.amazon.cn/	Public
Asia	Japan	Amazon.co.jp	https://affiliate.amazon.co.jp/	Public
Asia	Singapore	Amazon.sg	https://affiliate-program.amazon.sg/	Public

Additional information about commission rates, affiliate window, payment mentors, etc. can be found here: https://geni.us/amznprogramguide

Appendix B -
Amazon.com Commission Rates for Onsite, Offsite, and Influencers

Appendix B - Amazon.com Commission Rates

The commission rates for the "Offsite" Associates Program and the Amazon Influencer Program are the same as of June, 2022.[41]

Table 1 – Fixed Standard Commission Income Rates for Specific Product Categories

Product Category	Fixed Commission Income Rates
Amazon Games	20.00%
Luxury Beauty, Luxury Stores Beauty, Amazon Explore	10.00%
Digital Music, Physical Music, Handmade, Digital Videos	5.00%
Physical Books, Kitchen, Automotive	4.50%
Amazon Fire Tablet Devices, Amazon Kindle Devices, Amazon Fashion Women's, Men's & Kids Private Label, Luxury Stores Fashion, Apparel, Amazon Cloud Cam Devices, Fire TV Edition Smart TVs, Amazon Fire TV Devices, Amazon Echo Devices, Ring Devices, Watches, Jewelry, Luggage, Shoes, and Handbags & Accessories	4.00%
Toys, Furniture, Home, Home Improvement, Lawn & Garden, Pets Products, Headphones, Beauty, Musical Instruments, Business & Industrial Supplies, Outdoors, Tools, Sports, Baby Products, Amazon Coins	3.00%
PC, PC Components, DVD & Blu-Ray	2.50%
Televisions, Digital Video Games	2.00%
Amazon Fresh, Physical Video Games & Video Game Consoles, Grocery, Health & Personal Care	1.00%
Gift Cards; Wireless Service Plans; Alcoholic Beverages; Digital Kindle Products purchased as a subscription; Food prepared and delivered from a restaurant; Amazon Appstore, Prime Now, or Amazon Pay Places	0.00%
All Other Categories	4.00%

---

[41] https://geni.us/amazoncomcommrates

Appendix B - Amazon.com Commission Rates

Commission rates, as of June 2022, for the Amazon "Onsite" Associates Program are lower[42] and only apply to Direct Qualifying Purchases[43].

Table A – Fixed Onsite Associates Program Commission Income for Direct Qualifying Purchases in specific Product Categories

Product Category	Fixed Commission Income Rates
Luxury Beauty, Luxury Stores Beauty, Amazon Coins	5.00%
Furniture, Home, Home Improvement, Lawn & Garden, Pets Products, Pantry	4.00%
Headphones, Beauty, Musical Instruments, Business & Industrial Supplies	3.00%
Outdoors, Tools	2.75%
Digital Music, Grocery, Physical Music, Handmade, Digital Videos	2.50%
Physical Books, Health & Personal Care, Sports, Kitchen, Automotive, Baby Products	2.25%
Amazon Fire Tablet Devices, Amazon Kindle Devices, Amazon Fashion Women's, Men's & Kids Private Label, Apparel, Amazon Cloud Cam Devices, Fire TV Edition Smart TVs, Amazon Fire TV Devices, Amazon Echo Devices, Ring Devices, Watches, Jewelry, Luggage, Shoes, and Handbags & Accessories	2.00%
Amazon Fresh, Toys	1.50%
PC, PC Components, DVD & Blu-Ray	1.25%
Televisions, Digital Video Games	1.00%
Physical Video Games & Video Game Consoles	0.50%
Gift Cards; Wireless Service Plans; Alcoholic Beverages; Digital Kindle Products purchased as a subscription; Food prepared and delivered from a restaurant; Amazon Appstore, Prime Now, Amazon Pay Places, or Prime Wardrobe Purchases	0.00%
All Other Categories	2.00%

---

[42] https://geni.us/amazoncomonsiterates
[43] https://geni.us/directvindirectqualify

Acknowledgements

Acknowledgements

Wow, turns out that writing and publishing a book is not possible without a community pitching in!

This book would not have been possible without the help, support, and guidance of the following people. I cannot thank them enough for all they've done, not only for this project, but for me. I can only hope that in my lifetime I'm able to pay forward all their kindness.

First, a huge hat tip to my team! To **Joey**, **Jules**, **Ezra**, and **Alejandro** -- thank you so much for taking the time to read the first draft from cover to cover then turn my manuscript red with helpful suggestions and edits. To **P**, **Shannon**, and **Steven** -- I'm so lucky to have such an awesome executive team, and close friends, with me every step of the way. To **Matt** for always having the excitement and skills to help me with a quick fix or search for the proverbial needle in the haystack. To the rest of our amazing **team**, for building (and maintaining!) the tools of my dreams.

Another massive thank you to **Leilani Han** for going deep down the rabbit hole with me and taking the job of a beta reader to the max. You truly are a master of Amazon Associates and your edits and feedback have been absolutely essential in turning this into a book we can be proud of!

Douglas Mapes absolutely deserves a huge thank you for the numerous sessions talking me through the nuances of the Associates Operating Agreement and Policies, taking the time to really understand what I'm trying to build and accomplish, and being a conduit.

Many many thanks to my other beta readers who have also been incredibly generous with their time and feedback. Their contributions have helped provide a much better, and wider, perception on numerous topics throughout the book as well as helped level me up as a reluctant author. Another huge round of thank yous to **Dustin**

Acknowledgements

Howes, Jeven Dovey, **John Brubaker**, **Chris Yates**, **Rachel Thompson**, **Adam Weiss**, **Chris Guthrie**, **Rob Schab**, **Doug Cunnington, Ben Faw**, and **Jane Reid**!

My family also deserves to be acknowledged for giving me the (quiet!) time and space to work on this project. It wouldn't have been possible without their never ending support and love. Thanks **Shannon**, **MacKenzie**, and **Arwyn**! It's also important to call out my dad, **Greg Lakes**, for showing me what the love of writing looks like and my mom, **Mary Lakes**, for teaching me what entrepreneurship was. And, of course, my little brother, **Cole Lakes**, for jumping in to help me out on various projects including my first book.

It's also essential to call out **all of our clients** across Geniuslink, Kit, and Booklinker. Thank you for your support over all those years! On so many levels, I wouldn't be here today without each and every one of you.

Made in the USA
Columbia, SC
25 September 2024